T0216945

SpringerBriefs in Computer Science

SpringerBriefs present concise summaries of cutting-edge research and practical applications across a wide spectrum of fields. Featuring compact volumes of 50 to 125 pages, the series covers a range of content from professional to academic.

Typical topics might include:

- A timely report of state-of-the art analytical techniques
- A bridge between new research results, as published in journal articles, and a contextual literature review
- A snapshot of a hot or emerging topic
- An in-depth case study or clinical example
- A presentation of core concepts that students must understand in order to make independent contributions

Briefs allow authors to present their ideas and readers to absorb them with minimal time investment. Briefs will be published as part of Springer's eBook collection, with millions of users worldwide. In addition, Briefs will be available for individual print and electronic purchase. Briefs are characterized by fast, global electronic dissemination, standard publishing contracts, easy-to-use manuscript preparation and formatting guidelines, and expedited production schedules. We aim for publication 8–12 weeks after acceptance. Both solicited and unsolicited manuscripts are considered for publication in this series.

Indexing: This series is indexed in Scopus, Ei-Compendex, and zbMATH

Pedro Mejia Alvarez • Ricardo J. Zavaleta Vazquez
Susana Ortega Cisneros • Raul E. Gonzalez Torres

Real-Time Database Systems

Fundamentals, Architectures and Applications

 Springer

Pedro Mejia Alvarez
CINVESTAV-Guadalajara
Zapopan, Mexico

Ricardo J. Zavaleta Vazquez
ORACLE de Mexico, MDC
Zapopan, Mexico

Susana Ortega Cisneros
CINVESTAV-Guadalajara
Zapopan, Mexico

Raul E. Gonzalez Torres
CINVESTAV-Guadalajara
Zapopan, Mexico

ISSN 2191-5768   ISSN 2191-5776   (electronic)
SpringerBriefs in Computer Science
ISBN 978-3-031-44229-2   ISBN 978-3-031-44230-8   (eBook)
https://doi.org/10.1007/978-3-031-44230-8

This Springer imprint is published by the registered company Springer Nature Switzerland AG
The registered company address is: Gewerbestrasse 11, 6330 Cham, Switzerland

Paper in this product is recyclable.

Preface

A real-time database uses real-time processing to handle workloads whose state is constantly changing. This differs from traditional databases that contain persistent data, which are mostly unaffected by time. For example, a stock market changes very rapidly and is dynamic. As a result, the stock graphs of the different markets appear to be very unstable, yet a database must keep track of the current values of the market (e.g., New York Stock Exchange). Real-time processing means that a transaction is processed fast enough for the result to come back and be acted upon immediately (i.e., based on a deadline). Real-time databases are helpful for accounting, banking, law, medical records, multimedia, process control, reservation systems, scientific data analysis, and many other applications.

Big Data applications have initiated much research to develop systems supporting low-latency execution and real-time data analytics. Unfortunately, due to the high access latency to hard disks, existing disk-based systems can offer only offer soft real-time responses. The low performance is now also becoming an obstacle for organizations providing a real-time service (e.g., real-time bidding, advertising, social gaming). For instance, trading companies must detect sudden changes in the trading prices and react instantly (in several milliseconds), which is difficult to achieve using traditional disk-based processing-storage systems. Therefore, to meet the strict (hard) real-time requirements for analyzing mass amounts of data and servicing requests within milliseconds, an in-memory database system is necessary to keep the data in the random access memory (RAM) all the time.

These emergent applications (like big data) and classic ones (like industrial control systems) are data-driven, meaning that critical decisions are based on the analysis and interpretation of collected data. Moreover, under some circumstances (e.g., contact tracing during a pandemic), this data processing must be performed in a timely fashion.

The book is organized into four main sections:

1. **An Overview of Real-Time Database Systems**: Here, we delve into the realm of RTDBS. We discuss the specific requirements, transaction models, and scheduling algorithms that set RTDBS apart from conventional DBMS.

2. **Experimental Real-Time Databases**: This section presents various experimental RTDBS developed in academia with their architectures, features, and implementations. Experimental real-time database systems refer to database management systems (DBMS) that are developed and implemented for research purposes to explore and evaluate novel techniques, algorithms, and approaches in handling real-time data. These systems are not typically intended for production environments but serve as testbeds for researchers and developers to investigate and validate new ideas, algorithms, and architectures.
3. **Commercial Real-Time Databases**: This section presents various commercial RTDBS with their architectures, features, and implementations. Commercial real-time database systems refer to database management systems (DBMS) that are developed and offered by commercial vendors as products or services. These systems are designed to meet the requirements of real-time data processing and management in various industries and domains. Unlike experimental systems, commercial real-time database systems are intended for production environments and are backed by professional support, maintenance, and ongoing development.
4. **Applications of Real-Time Database Systems**: The final section showcases various applications of RTDBS across different domains, highlighting the versatility and necessity of RTDBS in the contemporary world.

This book encapsulates the vast expanse of RTDBS, providing a systematic approach to understanding, designing, and implementing them. Whether you are a student, a researcher, a software professional, or a technology enthusiast, we hope this book helps your path in exploring Real-Time Database Systems.

CINVESTAV-Guadalajara, Mexico   *Pedro Mejia-Alvarez*
Oracle-MDC, Zapopan, Jalisco, Mexico,   *Ricardo Zavaleta-Vazquez*
CINVESTAV-Guadalajara, Mexico   *Susana Ortega-Cisneros*
CINVESTAV-Guadalajara, Mexico   *Raul. E. Gonzalez-Torres*

Contents

Chapter 1
An Overview of Real-Time Database Systems

Real-Time Database Systems (RTDBS) emerge from the convergence of real-time systems and database systems. As real-time systems become more complex and require the management of a growing volume of information, incorporating databases becomes necessary. However, conventional database systems may not adequately support the timing and temporal requirements. RTDBS offers a solution to this issue by maintaining the integrity of the database and meeting the urgency of transaction execution.

This chapter provides a detailed exploration of real-time database systems specifically designed to handle data in real-time environments where timing constraints are crucial. The chapter begins by introducing the concept of real-time database systems, highlighting the unique challenges they face compared to conventional database systems. It explores the distinction between soft and hard real-time database systems, emphasizing the criticality of meeting strict timing requirements in hard real-time scenarios.

Characterizing real-time database systems is a key focus of this chapter. It discusses the essential characteristics that distinguish them from other database systems, such as predictability, responsiveness, and consistency. Furthermore, the chapter draws a contrast between real-time and conventional database systems, emphasizing the additional considerations and complexities introduced by real-time requirements. The real-time database model is examined in detail, focusing on data and consistency management aspects. It also covers real-time database system transactions and their significance in ensuring data integrity and timeliness. The chapter further explores transaction and query processing in real-time environments, including scheduling real-time transactions to meet timing constraints.

Admission control, a critical component of real-time database systems, is discussed to highlight its role in managing system resources and ensuring the timely execution of transactions. Concurrency control mechanisms are examined, addressing the challenges of data access and conflict resolution in real-time settings. The chapter also explores real-time distributed databases and the commit protocols required to maintain consistency across distributed environments. Recovery mechanisms specific to real-time database management systems are covered, focusing

P. Mejia Alvarez et al., *Real-Time Database Systems*, SpringerBriefs in Computer Science, https://doi.org/10.1007/978-3-031-44230-8_1

on the ability to recover from failures while adhering to timing constraints. Other important aspects covered in the chapter include input/output scheduling, which ensures timely data transfer between the database and external devices, and buffer management to optimize data storage and retrieval operations.

1.1 Challenges in Real-Time Database Systems

Real-Time Database Systems (RTDBS) are designed to handle time-constrained data and transactions, which require timely and predictable responses to meet deadlines. These systems are employed in various domains, including industrial control, financial services, and telecommunication networks [79]. However, numerous challenges arise when designing and implementing RTDBS. In this section, we discuss some of the primary challenges related to concurrency control, data consistency, and recovery mechanisms in RTDBS.

1. **Concurrency Control**: Concurrency control is crucial in RTDBS to ensure data consistency and transaction isolation while allowing multiple transactions to execute simultaneously [39]. Unfortunately, traditional concurrency control techniques, such as two-phase locking (2PL) and timestamp-based methods, can lead to priority inversion and unbounded blocking times, which are unsuitable for real-time applications. To overcome these limitations, researchers have proposed various real-time concurrency control techniques like priority inheritance, priority ceiling, and optimistic concurrency control [4, 36, 90]. However, these techniques may still experience challenges, such as increased transaction abort rates and complex implementation, which affect the system's predictability and performance.
2. **Data Consistency and Temporal Constraints**: Maintaining data consistency and addressing temporal constraints are significant challenges in RTDBS. While traditional databases focus on maintaining consistency through serializability, this notion may not be suitable for real-time applications due to the strict timing requirements [35]. To ensure timely data access, researchers have proposed alternative consistency models, such as epsilon serializability, probabilistic serializability, and real-time serializability [15, 76, 98]. These models aim to relax the consistency requirements and provide a trade-off between data freshness and response time.
3. **Recovery Mechanisms**: Recovery mechanisms in RTDBS must guarantee data durability and system availability while minimizing the impact on ongoing transactions [7]. Traditional recovery techniques, such as logging and checkpointing, may not be directly applicable to real-time systems due to their sequential nature and lack of time awareness. Researchers have proposed real-time logging and recovery algorithms, such as SPLIT and ARUN [96], which divide the data into equivalence classes based on transaction and data attributes. These algorithms allow for partial recovery, reducing the recovery time and enabling transactions to proceed without waiting for the entire system to recover.

As real-time applications become more complex and diverse, new challenges emerge in the design and implementation of RTDBS. For example, integrating emerging technologies, such as solid-state disks (SSDs) and non-volatile memory, can improve the performance and predictability of RTDBS [33]. Additionally, developing adaptive and self-tuning database systems that can dynamically adjust their behavior based on workload characteristics and system requirements is a promising research direction [50].

1.2 Soft vs. Hard Real-Time Database Systems

Speed is a selling point in everything, from cars to meal delivery to data management. The term real-time has been used by most in the database system industry to mean fast. For example, real-time processing enables more-or-less immediate results versus the previous century's typical overnight batch processing. However, a difference must be noted between real-time processing and real-time systems. In the latter, real-time means "various operations . . . that must guarantee response times within a specified time (deadline)". A fast database is suitable for real-time processing, but a real-time database aware of deadlines is required for real-time systems. It should also be noted that there is a crucial distinction between soft and hard real-time systems and the need for speed.

A soft real-time system wants speed and reliability and for all tasks to complete within the developer's scheduled window. Faster is usually better, but a missed deadline is not a life-or-death matter. One such example is voice-over IP or VoIP. If a task runs past its deadline, it might result in poor call quality or even a dropped call. It might feel essential and frustrating to the telemarketer on the phone, but the entire system doesn't fail, and no lives are lost.

The complete system failure of a soft real-time system is averted because a soft real-time system has the luxury of tolerating missed deadlines. A hard real-time database system must enforce set transaction deadlines without fail. Speed might be desirable, but it is not a necessity. Ultra-fast might feel fun when test-driving a new sports car, but is it fast enough to apply the brakes and avoid hitting that pedestrian who was texting instead of looking at the crossing light? Most would prefer a braking system with guaranteed deadlines and therefore guaranteed response time under such circumstances.

Hard real-time database system transactions are only allowed if they finish within their deadline. Transactions destined to be late are identified, interrupted, and forced to initiate rollback in time to satisfy deadlines. The real-time database system's goal is not to ensure speed (that is the purview of the real-time system developer that determines appropriate deadlines) but to maximize the number of transactions that meet their deadline. Speed can kill without a firm deadline for transaction rollback or commit. Or, to put it another way, speed is only good under certain circumstances if you have reliable brakes.

1.3 Contrast with Conventional Database Systems

The designer of a Real-Time Data Base System, such as the ones mentioned previously, might be tempted to use a traditional database management system as the backend. However, since its beginning, the term *Real-Time* has been a subject of misconceptions. Therefore, it is worth taking just a moment to enumerate some differences between real-time and conventional databases. In 1988, Stankovic noticed this situation and wrote a paper to clarify. In [103], he states that the results in the area we have today were possible thanks to the precise definition of the concept of a real-time system. By 1999, Stankovic also mentioned that the area of Real-Time databases was similar to the one we had in 1989 regarding Real-Time Systems. So, a new paper was required to shed some light on what a real-time database was. The following paragraphs summarize some crucial differences between these two flavors of database systems. One initial difference is this: in contrast to conventional database systems, RTDBS must often deal with an external environment that imposes new relations between the data objects in the database and the dynamic real-world objects they model.

The relation to the external environment introduces new consistency constraints besides the internal constraints in traditional databases [52] [55] [61]. These consistency restrictions are the *temporal* restrictions discussed in the previous section. In other words, we have two types of restrictions: on the one hand, stock index information in the database of a stock trading system must be sufficiently kept up to date. On the other hand, we have restrictions like the values of two data objects, such as the ones involved in the position of a vehicle, which must be sufficiently correlated in time.

Other challenges also arise. For example, one misconception is that advances in hardware will take care of the requirements of the real-time systems and the real-time databases [103]. However, advances in hardware will not ensure that real-time transactions be adequately scheduled to meet their deadlines. Similarly, they will only ensure that the data used is temporarily valid. Furthermore, more than faster hardware will be needed to solve the challenges of real-time transactions. Real-Time is about something apart from being fast but having a predictable response time. Fast computing only minimizes the average response time.

Advances in database technology are not enough, either. Real-Time transactions require time-cognizant protocols for concurrency control, committing, and transaction scheduling. Even with the popularity of in-memory databases, the challenges of real-time transactions will not be solved because disk access is only one source of unpredictability. Given these ideas, it is evident that studying real-time databases as a problem is required. Of course, we can take advantage of modern hardware or modern operating systems techniques. Still, it is essential to keep in mind that the area of real-time database systems has its problems and must be dealt with separately.

1.4 Real-Time Database Model

Real-time systems consist of two main components: the controlling system and the controlled system [63]. The controlled system is the environment that interacts with the computer and its software. In contrast, the controlling system interacts with its environment based on data collected from various sensors, such as distance and speed sensors. Therefore, the state of the environment must align with its current state with a high degree of precision. Otherwise, the actions taken by the controlling systems could lead to disastrous outcomes. Thus, it is necessary to monitor the environment in real-time and promptly process the information gathered from it. Often, the data collected is processed to generate new data.

This section explores the characteristics of data and transactions in real-time database systems.

1.4.1 Data and Consistency

Timing constraints in real-time database systems arise from the continuous need to monitor the environment and the necessity to supply data to the controlling system for its decision-making activities. The need to maintain consistency between the actual state of the environment and the state depicted by the contents of the database gives rise to the concept of temporal consistency. Temporal consistency comprises two elements:

- **Absolute consistency**: This consistency implies that data remains valid only between absolute points in time. It is necessary to maintain database consistency with the environment.
- **Relative consistency**: This consistency suggests that different data items used to generate new data must be temporally consistent with each other. A set of data items used to produce a new data item must form a relative consistency set R. A data item d is considered temporally consistent if and only if it is absolutely consistent and relatively consistent.

Each data item in a real-time database contains the object's current state (i.e., the current value stored in that data item) and two timestamps. These timestamps indicate the time when the committed transaction last accessed this data item. These timestamps are utilized in the concurrency control method to ensure that the transaction only reads from committed transactions and writes after the most recent committed write. Formally,

Definition 2.1 A data item in the real-time database is represented as:

$$d : (value, RTS, WTS, avi) \tag{1.1}$$

where d_{value} indicates the current state of d, d_{RTS} shows when the last committed transaction read the current state of d, d_{WTS} denoted when the previous committed transaction wrote d, i.e., when the observation relating to d was made, and d_{avi} represents d's absolute validity interval, i.e., the length of the time interval following R_{WTS} during which d is considered to be absolutely valid.

A set of data items used to generate a new data item forms a relative consistency set R. Each such set R is linked to a relative validity interval.

An individual data item is part of a relative consistency set, R, which is associated with a relative validity interval. For a data item $d \in R$, it is considered to have a correct state only when:

1. The value of d is logically consistent, meaning it satisfies all the integrity constraints.
2. The data item d is temporally consistent, which further breaks down into two criteria:

   - A data item $d \in R$ is deemed absolutely consistent if and only if the difference between the current time and the time of observation of d is less than or equal to the absolute validity interval of d.
   - Data items are relatively consistent if and only if for all $d' \in R$, the absolute difference between the timestamps of d and d' is less than or equal to the relative validity interval of R.

In simpler terms, every data item in a real-time database has a specific current state value along with two timestamps. These timestamps record when the last transaction that was committed accessed this data item. These timestamps significantly manage the system's concurrency, ensuring that transactions only read from other committed transactions and write after the latest committed write operation.

1.4.2 Real-Time Database System Transactions

This section discusses transactions in a real-time database system in terms of their data usage, time constraints, and the consequences of not meeting specified time constraints. A formal definition of transactions is required to analyze transactions and the correctness of management algorithms. For simplicity, it is assumed that each transaction reads and writes a data item at most once. From now on, r, w, a, and c represent read, write, abort, and commit operations, respectively.

Definition 2.2: A transaction T_i is a partial order with an ordering relation $\prec_i$ where:

1. $T_i = r_i(x), w_i(x) \mid x$ is a data item $\cup\, a_i, c_i$;
2. $a_i \in T_i$ if and only if $c_i \notin T_i$;
3. If t is c_i or a_i, for any other operation $p \in T_i$, $p \prec_i t$; and
4. If $r_i[x], w_i[x] \in T_i$, then either $r_i[x] \prec_i w_i[x]$ or $w_i[x] \prec_i r_i[x]$.

A transaction is a subset of read, write, and abort or commit operations. If the transaction executes an abort operation, it will not execute a commit operation. If a particular operation t is aborted or committed, the ordering relation dictates that all other operations precede the operation t in the execution of the transaction. If both read and write operations are executed on the same data item, the ordering relation defines the order between these operations.

A real-time transaction is a transaction with additional real-time attributes, such as timing constraints, criticalness, value function, unfinished work after the deadline, computation already executed, slackness, resource requirements, expected execution time, data requirements, periodicity, time of occurrence of events, and other semantics like transaction type (read-only, write-only, etc.). Based on the values of these attributes and the availability of information, real-time transactions can be characterized as having implications of missing deadlines (hard, critical, or soft real-time), arrival patterns (periodic, sporadic, or aperiodic), data access patterns (predefined or random), data requirements (known or unknown), runtime requirements (known or unknown), and accessed data types (continuous, discrete, or both). The most used parameters for real-time transaction scheduling algorithms are deadlines and criticality, which are often in conflict. This section discusses scheduling techniques found in the literature and how to determine which tasks are eligible for service, and how to assign priorities.

The first decision a scheduler must make is determining which transactions are eligible for execution. Transactions can be divided into two sets: eligible and non-eligible. The system could choose one of the following three alternatives:

- All jobs are eligible for service.
- Only non-tardy transactions are eligible for service.
- Only jobs with feasible transactions are eligible for service.

These three possibilities require increasing information about the transactions. For example, knowing which transactions are feasible requires knowledge about execution time or response time. Priorities must be assigned once the system knows which jobs can be executed. The real-time database system employs three types of transactions: write-only item transactions, update transactions, and read-only Transaction processing and concurrency control. A real-time database system should prioritize the criticalness of the transactions. However, when used in a real-time environment, traditional methods for transaction processing and concurrency control can lead to undesired behaviors. Below are four typified problems where priority signifies either the scheduling priority or criticality of the transaction:

- **Wasted wait**: This happens when a lower priority transaction waits for the commit of a higher priority transaction, and later the higher priority transaction is discarded due to missing its deadline.
- **Wasted restart**: This occurs when a higher priority transaction aborts a lower priority transaction, and later the higher priority transaction is discarded due to missing its deadline.
- **Unnecessary restart**: This occurs when a transaction in the validation phase is restarted despite history being serializable.

- **Wasted execution**: This situation arises when a lower-priority transaction in the validation phase is restarted due to a conflicting higher-priority transaction that hasn't finished yet.

Traditional two-phase locking methods suffer from the problems of wasted restart and wasted wait. In contrast, optimistic methods struggle with the issues of wasted execution and unnecessary restart.

1.5 Real-Time Database System: Transaction and Query Processing

In this section, we delve into transaction and query processing aspects and their various characteristics. Transactions and queries possess time constraints, and failing to meet these constraints can lead to a wide range of consequences [65]. Therefore, predictability is a critical factor in transaction processing [71]. For example, missing a deadline for a real-time transaction could result in catastrophic consequences, making it essential to ensure that such transactions are completed within the specified deadlines. Achieving this goal requires predicting the worst-case execution time and understanding the transaction's data and resource demands.

Unpredictability in database systems can arise from multiple sources [65]:

- The transaction's execution order depends on data values.
- Conflicts related to data and resources. Dynamic item paging and I/O operations.
- Transaction aborts, leading to rollbacks and restarts.
- Communication delays and site failures in distributed databases.

The execution route of a transaction may rely on the accessed data items, complicating worst-case execution time predictions. Refraining from using unbounded loops, recursive, or dynamically created data structures in real-time transactions is also advisable. Employing main memory databases can help mitigate the unpredictability of dynamic paging and I/O [52]. Additionally, deadlines and priority-driven I/O controllers (e.g., [99, 111]) can help reduce I/O unpredictability. Transaction rollbacks contribute to unpredictability, and it is thus advisable to limit a transaction to writing only within its memory area. Once the transaction is confirmed to commit, the modifications can be reported to the database [54].

1.5.1 Scheduling Real-Time Transactions

Real-time database system transactions are distinct due to their time constraints. While the performance goal in a conventional database system often focuses on average response time, the objective in an RTDBS is to minimize transactions that breach timing constraints [3]. The Timely Transactions Per Second (TTPS) metric demonstrates this aim [48].

Real-time job scheduling research primarily addresses CPU scheduling, but transaction scheduling involves additional resources. The following equation represents transaction execution time:

$$t_{exec} = t_{db} + t_{I/O} + t_{int} + t_{appl} + t_{comm} \qquad (1.2)$$

Where: t_{db} signifies DB operations processing $t_{I/O}$ denotes I/O processing t_{int} represents transaction interference t_{appl} refers to non-DB application processing t_{comm} is the communication time

Predictability is crucial for real-time transaction processing [63]. The above equation highlights various unpredictability sources, such as data and resource conflicts among transactions, dynamic paging, and I/O operations; the transaction aborts, leading to rollbacks and restarts, and more. Managing these sources of unpredictability is a complex and challenging task.

Scheduling policies significantly impact database system performance as they determine individual transaction priority selection [3]. Ramamritham elaborates in [78] on applying various scheduling techniques to different RTDBS types. He differentiates between hard and soft real-time systems and attempts to frame the real-time transactions problem as a generic real-time scheduling issue. He proposes that scheduling hard real-time transactions necessitates knowing when transactions are likely to be invoked. This information is readily available for periodic transactions. Still, an alternative approach may be required for aperiodic transactions, such as considering the smallest separation between two consecutive invocations as the period. Other essential information includes deadlines and worst-case execution times. Armed with this information, we can employ table-driven schedulers or preemptive priority-driven schedulers. It is crucial to ensure that the worst-case execution time exhibits minimal variance, as any variance will influence the generated schedule, possibly leading to extensive idle times between executions.

A transaction scheduling policy defines the priorities assigned to individual transactions [99]. The goal of transaction scheduling is to guarantee that as many transactions as possible meet their deadlines. Numerous transaction scheduling policies exist in the literature, but only a few are discussed here. Real-time database transactions can often be compared to tasks in a real-time system [99]. Scheduling involves allocating resources and time to tasks to fulfill specific performance requirements. A typical real-time system comprises multiple tasks that require concurrent execution. Each task has a value, representing the gain for the system if the task is completed within a specific time frame. Each task also has a deadline, specifying the time limit beyond which the computation result is considered worthless.

This discussion classifies transactions as hard, soft, and firm [99]. This classification reflects the value the system gains when a transaction meets its deadline. In systems using priority-driven scheduling algorithms, the value and deadline are employed to determine the priority [12].

Most real-time scheduling algorithms adopt priority-based scheduling [99]. In this context, transactions are assigned priorities based on their deadlines, criticality, or both. The criticality of a transaction indicates its level of importance. However, these two criteria may sometimes conflict. For example, transactions with short deadlines might not be critical, and vice versa. In such cases, transaction criticality is used instead of the deadline when selecting the appropriate priority value. This approach avoids the dilemmas of priority scheduling while integrating criticality and deadline to ensure that more critical transactions also meet their deadlines. The objective is to maximize the net worth of executed transactions for the system.

Different types of value functions can be associated with transactions, but the following simple functions are most common:

- Hard deadline transactions could result in disastrous consequences if the deadline is missed. In these cases, it can be argued that a large negative value is added to the system if a hard deadline is missed. These are usually safety-critical activities, such as those addressing life-threatening or environmental emergencies.
- Soft deadline transactions maintain some value even beyond their deadlines. Typically, the value drops to zero at some point after the deadline.
- Firm deadline transactions add no value to the system once their deadlines expire; in other words, the value drops to zero at the deadline.

1.6 Admission Control

Real-time database management systems (RTDBMS) are designed to handle time-critical applications that require strict timing constraints and deadlines for data transactions. One of the essential components of an RTDBMS is admission control, which is responsible for deciding whether to accept or reject incoming transactions based on their temporal requirements and the current system workload. This section presents an overview of admission control in real-time database management systems, discussing various techniques, examples, and equations relevant to the topic.

Several admission control techniques have been proposed for use in RTDBMS. Some of the most common approaches include the following.

- **Static Admission Control**:
  In static admission control, the decision to accept or reject a transaction is made based on the system's design-time parameters, such as the maximum number of concurrent transactions and the worst-case execution time for each transaction type. A typical static admission control approach is to use the utilization control algorithm, which can be expressed as:

$$U(n) = \sum_{i=1}^{n} \frac{C_i}{T_i} \leq n \cdot (2^{\frac{1}{n}} - 1), \tag{1.3}$$

where $U(n)$ is the system's total utilization, n is the number of tasks, C_i is the worst-case execution time of task i, and T_i is the period of task i [64].

- **Dynamic Admission Control**:
  Dynamic admission control makes decisions based on runtime parameters and system state. In addition, it considers factors such as current workload, deadlines, and resource availability. Examples of dynamic admission control techniques include the EDF-based (Earliest Deadline First) admission control [105], and the IMpact-Based Admission Control (IMPAC) [117]. The EDF-based admission control calculates the slack time (ST) for each incoming transaction, defined as the difference between the transaction's deadline and its estimated completion time. If the slack time is positive, the transaction is accepted, and if it is negative, the transaction is rejected:

$$ST_i = D_i - (E_i + S_i), \tag{1.4}$$

  where ST_i is the slack time for transaction i, D_i is the deadline of transaction i, E_i is the estimated completion time of transaction i, and S_i is the start time of transaction i.
  The Impact method, on the other hand, computes an impact factor for each transaction based on the degree to which it may affect the timeliness of other transactions in the system. The impact factor (IF) is calculated as:

$$IF_i = \sum_{j \in ConflictingTransactions(i)} \frac{W_i \cdot C_j}{D_j - E_j}, \tag{1.5}$$

  where IF_i is the impact factor of transaction i, W_i is the weight of transaction i, C_j is the execution time of transaction j, D_j is the deadline of transaction j, and E_j is the estimated completion time of transaction j. A transaction is accepted if its impact factor is lower than a pre-defined threshold.
- **Hybrid Admission Control**:
  Hybrid admission control techniques combine the strengths of both static and dynamic approaches to provide more robust admission control decisions. One such approach is the Predictive Dynamic Real-Time Admission Control (PDR-TAC) [74]. This method uses a prediction model to estimate future system workload, taking into account both historical and current workloads. Based on the predicted workload and available resources, the algorithm dynamically decides whether to accept or reject a transaction.
  One recent example of **Admission Control** can be found in [48]. Kang et al. define a *degree of timing constraint violation*, δ, which is calculated periodically using the following formula:

$$\delta(k) = \frac{t_m(k) - t_s}{t_s} \tag{1.6}$$

  where k refers to the measurement period, t_m refers to the average service delay and t_s is the desired delay bound. Depending on the workload, the calculated $\delta(k)$ may vary abruptly. A smoother value can be obtained by using an exponential moving average over several measurement periods:

$$\delta_s(k) = \alpha \cdot \delta(k) + (1 - \alpha) \cdot \delta_{s-1}(k) \qquad (1.7)$$

where $0 \le \alpha \le 1$ is a parameter in the system, but in [48] a value of $\alpha = 0.5$ is used. Notice that a smaller α implies considering a longer history of δs, while $\alpha = 1$ implies using only the current value of δ.

1.7 Concurrency Control

In database systems, simultaneous access to database items by various transactions through *read* and *write* operations must be managed to maintain database consistency. **Concurrency Control** (CC) protocols address conflicts between transactions. These protocols ensure the correctness of an execution history by checking **Serializability**, which means the transaction output should be the same as if they were executed sequentially, one after another [14].

To develop a real-time transaction scheduling algorithm, two requirements must be met:

1. Defining transaction priorities
2. Resolving conflicts between transactions using parameters like deadline, criticality, slack time, etc.

Real-time databases have extensively studied concurrency control in literature. The challenge is balancing transaction urgency while maintaining system consistency. Traditional concurrency control protocols are unsuitable for real-time transactions due to frequent priority inversions [56]. Many time-aware concurrency controls have been proposed, often extending two-phase locking (2PL), timestamp, and optimistic concurrency control protocols.

1.7.1 Priority Inversion in Real-Time Transactions

The problem of priority inversion comes when a high priority transaction needs a lock held by a low priority transaction [51]. The regular 2PL protocol would let the high priority transaction wait until the low priority transaction releases the lock. For example, imagine the case where T_0 is blocked by T_3 for accessing some data object, then T_3 is blocked by T_2, and the priorities are such that $T_0 > T_2 > T_3$. In this situation, the high priority transaction might end up missing its deadline, impacting the performance metrics of the real-time database. Priority inversion is highly undesirable in real-time applications because the delay may become unbounded.

1.7.2 Locking Concurrency Control Protocols

Pessimistic concurrency control uses locks to synchronize concurrent actions. The most common protocol for traditional systems is Two-Phase Locking (2PL). 2PL blocks a requesting transaction if the data is already locked in an incompatible mode. In this protocol, all lock operations occur before the first unlock operation in the transaction. The phase where locks are obtained is the *expanding phase*, and the phase where locks are released is the *shrinking phase*. 2PL can be used in real-time transactions, but it has two main issues: deadlocks and priority inversion.

One initial solution for priority inversion is simply aborting the lower-priority transaction. This algorithm, shown in Algorithm 1, is called the **High-Priority Protocol**. In this case, there is no blocking, resulting in rapid resolution.

Algorithm 1 $HighPriority(T_R, T_H)$

---
if $pr(T_R) > pr(T_H)$ **then**
    T_R aborts T_H
else
    T_R waits
end if

The High-Priority protocol has two issues. First, aborting transactions wastes resources. Second, depending on the priority assignment function, an aborted trans-action may restart with a higher priority than before. For instance, if the system uses the *least slack* to assign priorities, the new incarnation of a transaction may have the least slack and, therefore, a higher priority. This problem is known as **cyclic restart**. The **High Priority without cyclic restart** protocol addresses this issue by also analyzing the priority of the future incarnation of the current holder transaction. The algorithm is listed in Algorithm 2.

Algorithm 2 $HighPriorityNoCyclicRestart(T_R, T_H)$

---
if $pr(T_R) > pr(T_H)$ AND $pr(T_R) > pr(T_R^A)$ **then**
    T_R aborts T_H
else
    T_R waits
end if

The system could be designed to execute the blocking transaction (low priority) with the priority of the blocked transaction (high priority) to avoid aborting the low-priority transaction. This is a way of reflecting the urgency of completing the low-priority transaction. This approach is called **Wait Promote**, and its pseudocode is shown in Algorithm 3. The advantage of this approach is that the intermediate blocking is eliminated. However, the system still blocks the high-priority transaction.

Algorithm 3 $WaitPromote(T_R, T_H)$

---

if $pr(T_R) > pr(T_H)$ **then**
    T_R waits
    T_H inherits the priority of T_R
else
    T_R waits
end if

Algorithm 4 $ConditionalRestart(T_R, T_H)$

E_H := estimated remaining running time of T_H
S_R := estimated slack time of T_R
if $pr(T_R) > pr(T_H)$ AND $pr(T_R) > pr(T_R^A)$ **then**
    if $S_R >= E_H$ **then**
        T_R waits
        T_H inherits the priority of T_R
    else
        T_R aborts T_H
    end if
else
    T_R waits
end if

Another option to deal with the priority inversion is to do a conditional restart of the low-priority transaction. The decision would be based on the estimated length of the transaction. In other words, the low-priority transaction could inherit the priority of the other only if it is close to completion; abort it otherwise. This approach is known as **Conditional Restart Protocol**. The pseudocode is shown in Algorithm 4. The problem with this idea is that estimates of transaction lengths must be available.

In [90], the RWPCP (Read-Write Priority Ceiling Protocol) is proposed as a pessimistic concurrency control protocol suitable for periodic hard real-time transactions. RWPCP is an extension of the PCP (Priority Ceiling Protocol). RWPCP proposes priority levels for writing and reading (WPL_i and RPL_i, respectively). WPL_i is the highest priority of all transactions that may write O_i. RPL_i is the highest priority of all transactions that may read or write O_i. The idea is that if a transaction wants to lock a data object O_i, its priority has to be greater than $RWPL_i$, where $RWPL_i$ is WPL_i if O_i is read-locked and it is APL_i if it is write-locked. If the transaction happens to have a priority greater than $RWPL_i$, then the priority of the blocking transaction is increased (i.e., it inherits the priority of the blocked transaction).

To understand $RWPCP$ better, let us review one example given in [56]. Suppose that we have 3 transactions T_1, T_2, and T_3 with priorities 1, 2, and 3, respectively. The lower the number, the higher the priority. Suppose also that T_1 reads object O_1, T_2 writes object O_1 and reads object O_2, and T_3 writes object O_2. This means that O_1 has $WPL_1 = 2$ and $APL_1 = 1$, according to the previous definition. O_2 has $WPL_2 = 3$ and $APL_2 = 2$. Figure 1.1 shows how the transactions would be executed.

T_3 write-locks object O_2 successfully and $RWPL_2 = WPL_2 = 2$. Then T_2 arrives and preempts T_3 because it has a higher priority, but it fails to acquire the write-lock on O_1 because it would require a priority higher than 2. T_3 later releases the lock for O_2 and T_2 is now able to acquire the write lock. At that point, $RWPL_1 = APL_1 = 1$. T_1 kicks in and preempts T_2 but fails to acquire the read lock for O_1 because it does not have a priority higher than 1. Later, T_2 acquires a read lock on object O_2 successfully. Once the locks on O_1 and O_2 are released by T_2, T_1 comes in, and it can now acquire the read lock on object O_1.

As mentioned earlier, this protocol is suitable for periodic hard real-time transactions. Still, it requires information about the set of possible transactions in the system and a fixed set of data objects. Also, notice that a high-priority transaction may, in some cases, be blocked for a long time. The advantage, though, is that it allows at most only one priority inversion for every transaction [91].

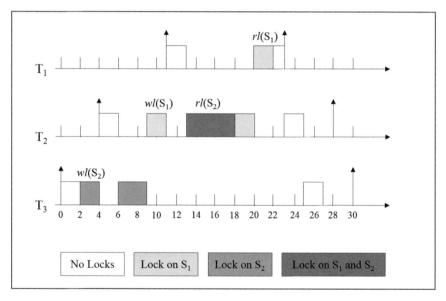

Fig. 1.1 Example of RWPCP Schedule [56]

2VPCP (Two-version priority ceiling protocol) [54] was proposed to reduce the time that high priority transactions are blocked. It uses the notion of a local and a consistent version of the data objects. Read operations read from the consistent version; write operations update the local versions; committed transactions update the consistent version. Before a transaction commits, it has to convert its write locks into "certify" locks. The certify locks grants the permission to update the consistent version of the data. For the case of 2VPCP, $RWPL_i = WPL_i$ when a transaction acquires a read or write lock. $RWPL_i = APL_i$ when a transaction acquires a certify lock. Let us see an example to understand the protocol better. Let us use the same set of transactions, objects, and priorities described before (See Figure 1.2).

T_3 acquires the write lock on O_2 successfully and $RWPL_2 = WPL_2 = 3$. T_2 then preempts T_3 and tries to acquire a write lock on O_1 and in this case it succeeds because it has a priority 2, which is higher than $RWPL_2 = 3$. Now $RWPL_1 = WPL_1 = 2$.

Later T_1 arrives and wants a read lock on O_1. Since it has a higher priority than $RWPL_1 = 2$ and $RWPL_2 = 3$, it acquires the lock successfully. Then T_1 unlocks the objects and commits. T_2 then wants to commit and has to acquire a certify lock for the written object O_1. It succeeds because the priority of the transaction is greater than $RWPL_2 = 3$. At that point, T_2 copies its local version to the consistent version. In this case, we can observe that low priority transactions do not block higher priority transactions because high priority transactions utilize the consistent version of the objects.

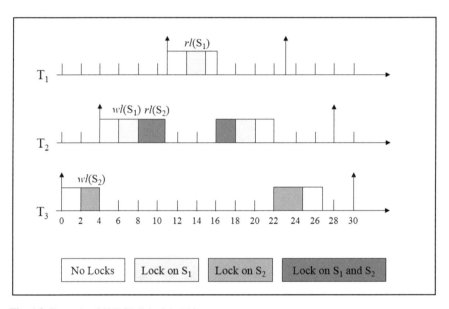

Fig. 1.2 Example of 2VPCP Schedule [56]

1.7.3 Optimistic Concurrency Control Protocols

We have previously discussed the Pessimistic approach to concurrency control. However, an optimistic method of handling concurrency exists, which we will discuss in this section.

Optimistic concurrency control protocols (OCC) are those where data conflicts are not checked during the execution of a transaction. A transaction executed under this model follows these phases:

1. **Read phase**: Retrieve values from the database and update local copies.

2. **Validation phase**: Conduct a backward or forward validation and execute a conflict resolution algorithm if needed.
3. **Write phase**: If validation is successful, write the local copies to the database. If not, discard updates and restart the transaction.

The validation step is the most intriguing part of an OCC protocol. As previously discussed, the concurrency control scheduler must find a serializable schedule. Therefore, an OCC protocol needs to ensure during the validation phase that if a transaction T_i is serialized before transaction T_j, this schedule satisfies the following two rules [38]:

1. **R/W rule.** Data items modified by T_i should not have been read by T_j at the time of the modification.
2. **W/W rule.** Modifications performed by T_j should not be overwritten by T_i.

If either of these rules are not met, one of the following conflict resolution options can be employed:

1. The first option is known as **Broadcasting commit**. This option does not consider priority. Instead, the transaction T always commits, and all conflicting transactions are aborted. This approach is inefficient in real-time databases due to the potential number of rollbacks.
2. The **Sacrifice Policy** (or **OPT-Sacrifice**) mandates that the transaction T that detects the conflict. However, there's no guarantee that the other transaction(s) will commit. If all transactions in the history abort, then T is unnecessarily aborted.
3. Another approach is to wait and see if the transactions in the history commit. If they do, transaction T must commit. This approach is known as **Wait Policy** (or **OPT-Wait**). The problem with waiting is that if the conflicting history's transactions commit, and if T it is a low-priority transaction, it may not have enough time to restart and commit. Moreover, the longer T stays around, the higher the likelihood of conflicts.
4. Another attempt to solve the problem is by allowing T to commit unless there is more than X percent of conflicting transactions. This approach is called **Wait-X Policy** (or **OPT-Wait-X**), and it is a compromise between sacrifice and wait.
   Wait-X can be seen as a generalization of OPT-Sacrifice and OPT-Wait policies. If $X = 0$, we get the sacrifice policy, whereas if $X = 100$, we get the Wait policy. [34] shows that $X = 50$ yields the best results.
5. Another example of an optimistic concurrency control protocol is provided in [62]. This protocol utilizes timestamp intervals, which are adjusted throughout the execution of the algorithm. If an interval is null at the end of a transaction, the transaction is aborted.
   The transactions are initially assigned a timestamp interval spanning $TI_i = [0, \infty)$. When another transaction executes, its validation phase, TI_i, is adjusted to reflect the data or access dependencies. The pseudocode of $validate()$ and $adjust()$ are shown in Algorithm 5 and Algorithm 6, respectively.

Algorithm 5 $validate(T_v)$

Select a $TS(T_v)$ from $TI(T_v)$ *
for all T_α in its read phase **do**
    $adjust(T_\alpha)$
end for
Read and write timestamps for data objects

Thus far, we have noticed that 2PL protocols suffer from unnecessary restarts and unproductive waits, while optimistic methods suffer from wasted execution and unnecessary restarts. However, optimistic protocols are non-blocking and deadlock-free. The question of which approach is superior remains open. Two studies on this topic have been conducted in the literature. In the first one [34], 2PL (High Priority) was compared against OCC (Broadcasting commit), and it was found that under the overload management policy of discarding tardy transactions, OCC can outperform 2PL. However, a 1991 study [38] compared 2PL vs. OCC (OCCL-SVW) and found that OCC outperforms 2PL when data contention is low; otherwise, 2PL outperforms OCC.

Algorithm 6 $adjust(T_\alpha)$

---

for all O_i in $RS(T_v)$ **do**
    if O_i in $WS(T_\alpha)$ **then**
        $TI(T_\alpha) = TI(T_\alpha) \cap [TS(T_v), \infty]$
    end if
    if $TI(T_\alpha == [\,]$ **then**
        restart T_α
    end if
end for
for all O_i in $WS(T_v)$ **do**
    if O_i in $RS(T_\alpha)$ **then**
        $TI(T_\alpha) = TI(T_\alpha) \cap [0, TS(T_v - 1)]$
    end if
    if O_i in $WS(T_\alpha)$ **then**
        $TI(T_\alpha) = TI(T_\alpha) \cap [TS(T_v), \infty]$
    end if
    if $TI(T_\alpha) == [\,]$ **then**
        restart T_α
    end if
end for

1.7.4 Comparison of Concurrency Control Protocols

Each concurrency control protocol has its advantages and disadvantages. For example, locking-based ensures serializability but may suffer performance issues due to lock contention and priority inversion. On the other hand, timestamp-based protocols, such as BTO, CTO, and OCC, allow transactions to execute concurrently without locks, leading to better performance in systems with low contention. However, these protocols may suffer from a high abort rate in systems with high contention.

When choosing a concurrency control protocol, it is essential to consider the specific requirements and characteristics of the system. Factors to consider include:

- The degree of contention: Systems with low contention may benefit from the optimistic approach of timestamp-based protocols, while systems with high contention may require the stricter control provided by locking-based protocols.
- Priority requirements: If priority scheduling is essential, consider using protocols that support priority-based conflict resolution, such as 2VPCP or CTO.
- Storage requirements: Protocols that require maintaining multiple versions of data objects, such as 2VPCP, may increase storage and complexity requirements.
- Performance and scalability: Locking-based protocols can suffer from performance issues due to lock contention, while timestamp-based protocols can offer better performance and scalability in certain situations.

In practice, many database systems employ a combination of concurrency control protocols to provide the best balance of performance, consistency, and isolation for the specific workload and system requirements. Additionally, modern database systems often include mechanisms for dynamically adjusting the concurrency control strategy based on the current system state and workload, further optimizing performance and resource utilization.

On the other hand, The choice between pessimistic and optimistic concurrency control protocols depends on a real-time database system's specific requirements and environment. For example, pessimistic protocols, such as 2PL, can be more suitable for high data contention scenarios. In contrast, optimistic protocols, like OCC, can be advantageous when data contention is low or the system requires a deadlock-free and non-blocking approach. Both methods have their strengths and weaknesses. Pessimistic approaches can result in unnecessary restarts and unproductive waits, while optimistic methods can suffer from wasted execution and unnecessary restarts. Ultimately, the decision should be based on analyzing the system's requirements, workload, and performance expectations. By understanding the trade-offs involved, designers can select the most appropriate concurrency control protocol to achieve the desired consistency, efficiency, and reliability level in a real-time database system.

1.7.5 Deadlocks in Concurrency Control Protocols

Deadlocks represent another common issue in concurrency control protocols, arising when a group of transactions is caught in a circular wait. Consider the example in Figure 1.3, where three transactions block each other: Transaction 1 requires a lock on object O_2, which is held by Transaction 2. Thus, Transaction 1 must wait for Transaction 2 to complete. However, Transaction 2 is also waiting for Transaction 3 to release a lock on object O_3. Similarly, Transaction 3 is unable to release the lock on object O_3 until it locks O_1.

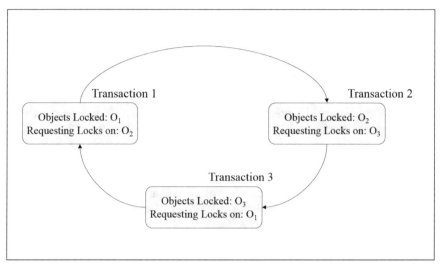

Fig. 1.3 Example of a deadlock between 3 transactions

Various solutions exist to address this situation, with the fundamental idea being that the system must select one transaction to abort. In the example above, breaking the cycle resolves the issue, transforming the problem into one of choosing the best transaction to abort. Some options include:

- Aborting the transaction that has exceeded its deadline.
- Aborting the transaction with the most distant deadline.
- Aborting the least important transaction.

Notably, deadlocks usually involve two transactions, as mentioned in [24]. As a result, implementing a straightforward deadlock-breaking protocol could be more beneficial, as proposed by [51].

1.8 Real-Time Distributed Databases and Commit Protocols

Commit protocols play a critical role in ensuring data consistency and concurrency control in RTDDBs. They are responsible for coordinating the actions of distributed transactions and guaranteeing that either all the changes are committed or none are committed in case of failure. The most widely used commit protocol in traditional distributed databases is the two-phase commit (2PC) protocol [32]. However, the 2PC protocol is unsuitable for RTDDBs because it needs to consider the time constraints and dynamic workloads inherent in real-time systems [37].

To address the limitations of the 2PC protocol, researchers have proposed various real-time commit protocols that consider the timing requirements and other characteristics of RTDDBs. Some prominent real-time commit protocols include:

- **Real-time Two-Phase Commit (RT-2PC):** This protocol extends the traditional 2PC protocol by introducing timing constraints and priority-based scheduling of commit processing [41]. RT-2PC protocol uses a coordinator to manage the commit process and ensure that higher-priority transactions are processed before lower-priority ones. The coordinator also aborts transactions that cannot be completed within their deadline to ensure the timely completion of higher-priority transactions [100].
- **Real-time Optimistic Commit Protocol (ROCP):** ROCP is an optimistic commit protocol that assumes conflicts are rare and uses timestamps to detect and resolve conflicts during the commit phase [102]. ROCP involves three phases: the read phase, the validation phase, and the write phase. During the read phase, transactions read data items without acquiring locks. In the validation phase, transactions check for conflicts and determine whether they can commit. Finally, the write phase is responsible for making the changes permanent. As a result, ROCP has the advantage of lower communication overhead and better concurrency compared to 2PC-based approaches [102].
- **Priority-Based Commit Protocol (PBCP):** PBCP is a commit protocol that prioritizes transactions based on their deadlines and uses a decentralized approach to reduce communication overhead and improve performance [57]. PBCP eliminates the need for a central coordinator and allows transactions to commit or abort independently, based on local decisions at each site. This decentralized approach reduces the likelihood of contention and prioritizes transactions with tight deadlines. PBCP has been shown to improve system performance and reduce the number of aborted transactions in RTDDBs [57].
- **Real-time Three-Phase Commit Protocol (RT-3PC):** The RT-3PC protocol extends the traditional Three-Phase Commit (3PC) protocol by incorporating timing constraints and dynamic priority assignment [29]. In RT-3PC, transactions are assigned priorities based on their deadlines, and these priorities are dynamically adjusted during the commit process to ensure that transactions with tighter deadlines receive preferential treatment. RT-3PC has the advantage of being non-blocking, which means that the protocol can continue to make progress even in the presence of failures [29].

Real-time distributed databases face the challenge of meeting stringent timing requirements while ensuring data consistency and concurrency control in a distributed environment. Commit protocols are an essential component of RTDDBs, responsible for coordinating the actions of distributed transactions and ensuring data consistency. Researchers have proposed various real-time commit protocols, such as RT-2PC, ROCP, PBCP, and RT-3PC, which consider the timing requirements and other characteristics of RTDDBs. The choice of a commit protocol in RTDDBs depends on factors such as workload characteristics, the frequency of conflicts, and the requirements for fault tolerance and performance. Each real-time commit protocol discussed above has its own set of advantages and trade-offs, making it suitable for different types of RTDDB applications. Therefore, it is essential for database designers and administrators to carefully evaluate the requirements of their real-time applications and choose the appropriate commit protocol to ensure the timely execution of transactions and maintain data consistency in their RTDDB systems.

As real-time applications continue to grow in importance and complexity, further research into real-time commit protocols and other aspects of RTDDBs is necessary to address the emerging challenges and requirements in this field. The future of real-time distributed databases and commit protocols lies in continuously exploring and developing new techniques to meet the ever-growing demands of real-time applications. Some potential research directions include:

- **Adaptive commit protocols:** Developing commit protocols that can adapt to the changing workloads and system conditions in real-time applications is crucial. These adaptive protocols can help improve the system's overall performance and resource utilization by dynamically adjusting the commit processing based on the current system state [1].
- **Machine learning-based commit protocols:** Machine learning techniques can be employed to predict transaction conflicts, resource utilization, and deadline violations. These predictions can be used to develop intelligent commit protocols that optimize the commit process and improve the performance of RTDDBs [119].
- **Fault-tolerant commit protocols:** Ensuring fault tolerance in real-time distributed databases is essential, as failures can lead to severe consequences in critical real-time applications. Developing commit protocols that efficiently handle failures and maintain system availability is an important research direction [42].

In conclusion, real-time distributed databases and commit protocols are critical components of many real-time applications. The continuous advancements in this field will help address the emerging challenges and requirements of modern real-time systems, ensuring that they can provide the necessary performance, consistency, and fault tolerance to support the demands of their applications.

1.9 Recovery in Real-Time Database Management Systems

Real-time database management systems (RTDBMS) are designed to handle time-critical applications that require strict timing constraints and deadlines for data transactions. In addition to satisfying these temporal requirements, RTDBMS must also ensure the consistency and durability of data in the face of failures. This section provides a comprehensive overview of recovery techniques in real-time database management systems.

Several recovery techniques have been proposed for use in RTDBMS. We will discuss each of these methods, considering the contributions of various researchers in the field.

1. **Logging-Based Recovery**: Logging-based recovery methods involve recording database changes in a log, which can be used to recover the database to a consistent state following a failure. One such logging-based technique is the Write-Ahead Logging (WAL) [32], which ensures that its associated log records are written to stable storage before a transaction is committed. The ARIES (Algorithm for Recovery and Isolation Exploiting Semantics) [69] is another well-known recovery method that uses logging and considers transaction semantics during recovery. This approach allows for fine-grained recovery actions and ensures that only the relevant portions of the log are processed during recovery.

2. **Checkpoint-Based Recovery**: Checkpoint-based recovery methods periodically create a snapshot of the database, known as a checkpoint, which is used as the starting point for recovery after a failure. Elmasri et al. [26] proposed a fuzzy checkpointing technique, which allows ongoing transactions to continue during the checkpointing process. This technique reduces the checkpointing overhead by minimizing the impact on transaction execution. Vrbsky and Liu [114] introduced a soft checkpointing approach for maintaining the consistency of the database during recovery, which involves periodically saving a consistent snapshot of the database without blocking transaction execution.

3. **Combined Recovery Methods**: Combined recovery methods integrate both logging and checkpointing techniques to achieve a balance between recovery time and I/O overhead. Ramamritham and Haritsa [79] introduced a two-level recovery mechanism that combines selective checkpointing and redoes logging to improve recovery efficiency. The Adaptive Recovery Technique (ART) proposed by Son and Krishna [101] dynamically adjusts the logging and checkpointing rates based on the system's workload and failure history.

4. **Concurrency Control Mechanism**: Ulusoy proposed a concurrency control mechanism called Deadline Oriented Concurrency Control (DOCC) that integrates recovery with the scheduling of real-time transactions [113]. This mechanism combines transaction scheduling and concurrency control to reduce the probability of deadline misses. In case of a failure, the DOCC mechanism uses logging to recover the state of the database to a consistent state.

5. **Epsilon Serializability**: Sivasankaran et al. [95] introduced Epsilon Serializability (ESR) is a relaxed consistency criterion for RTDBMS that can enhance recovery efficiency. ESR allows for a controlled level of inconsistency in the database to provide better concurrency and reduce the overhead of maintaining strict serializability. By tolerating a certain degree of inconsistency during recovery, the system can achieve faster recovery times and better overall performance.

6. **Real-Time Two-Phase Commit Protocol**: Shu et al. [94] developed a real-time variant of the traditional two-phase commit protocol (RT-2PC) to improve the recovery process in RTDBMS. The RT-2PC protocol incorporates time constraints and priorities to optimize the commit process and minimize the impact of failures on the system's performance. Furthermore, in case of failures, the RT-2PC protocol employs logging and coordination among participating nodes to ensure that the recovery process is efficient and the consistency of the distributed real-time database is maintained.

7. **Recovery Reintegration Framework**: DiPippo et al. [25] proposed a reintegration framework for real-time databases that focuses on the efficient reintegration of a failed node into a distributed RTDBMS. The framework aims to minimize the disruption of real-time transactions during recovery and maintain the system's overall performance. The reintegration process involves transferring data from a backup node to the failed node and synchronizing the state of the real-time database across all nodes.

8. **The Multi-version Concurrency Control Approach**: Abbott and Garcia-Molina [2] proposed a multi-version concurrency control approach that leverages multiple versions of data items to increase concurrency and facilitate recovery in RTDBMS. This approach allows transactions to access older versions of data items, thus reducing the need for rollback and improving the system's performance during recovery.

1.10 Input/Output Scheduling in Real-Time Database Systems

A key challenge in RTDBS is designing efficient Input/Output (I/O) scheduling algorithms that ensure timely data retrieval and storage. I/O scheduling is the process of determining the order and priority of data requests in a real-time database system. The main objective of I/O scheduling is to minimize the response time and meet the deadlines of transactions. The problem can be mathematically described as follows:

Given a set of transactions $T = \{T_1, T_2, ..., T_n\}$, where each transaction T_i has an arrival time a_i, a deadline d_i, and a set of data requests $R_i = \{r_{i1}, r_{i2}, ..., r_{im}\}$, the goal is to find an optimal I/O scheduling that satisfies the following constraints:

$$\min \sum_{i=1}^{n} \sum_{j=1}^{m} w_{ij}(C_{ij} - a_i) \tag{1.8}$$

$$\text{s.t. } C_{ij} \leq d_i, \forall i, j \tag{1.9}$$

Here, C_{ij} represents the completion time of request r_{ij}, and w_{ij} is a weight associated with request r_{ij} that can represent its relative importance. The objective function in (1) aims to minimize the total weighted completion time of all requests, while the constraint in (2) ensures that all requests are completed before their respective deadlines.

In a traditional disk-based database system, disk I/O is one activity that occupies most of the execution time. One reason for that comes from the seeking time because the disk head has to move to the appropriate disk sector or track to perform reads or writes. Let us see an example to understand better why this is a problem.

In Figure 1.4, the disk head is located in the track x of the disk, and there are four I/O requests in the queue. The question is in which direction should move the head. If the I/O requests are associated with a priority, then the head could choose to order

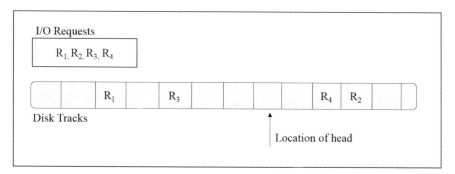

Fig. 1.4 Example of the disk head servicing four I/O requests

the request based on that priority (that is, using a High-Priority First Scheduling). Specifically, if we had that:

$$pr(R_1) > pr(R_2) > pr(R_3) > pr(R_4) \tag{1.10}$$

then one possible schedule is R_1, R_2, R_3 and R_4.

This schedule may not be acceptable, though, because it needs to consider the number of tracks the head has to traverse to attend to all four requests. In this example, the head would have to move 32 tracks.

In contrast, more straightforward scheduling like R_4, R_2, R_3, and R_1 would involve moving only through 11 tracks. This is the resulting schedule of the Elevator Algorithm. The idea is to move the head in one direction until all requests in such order are satisfied. Then the head can run in the opposite direction. Although, in this particular example, the Elevator Algorithm requires less movement, the resulting ordering considers the requests' priority. Notice that in this case, the algorithm attends the at the end.

Research on I/O scheduling in real-time database systems can be broadly classified in the following sections.

1.10.1 Feasible Deadline SCAN (FD-SCAN)

The Feasible Deadline SCAN (FD-SCAN) algorithm [81] is an extension of the EDF algorithm that considers the disk arm's current position and movement direction. This algorithm selects the request with the earliest deadline among those that can be serviced without violating the deadlines of other requests.

Example: Consider a disk with tracks numbered from 1 to 10 and data requests $R = \{r_1, r_2, r_3\}$ with track numbers $T_1 = 4$, $T_2 = 8$, and $T_3 = 2$ and deadlines $D_1 = 5$, $D_2 = 3$, and $D_3 = 7$, respectively. If the disk arm is currently at track 6 and moving towards the higher-numbered tracks, the FD-SCAN algorithm schedules the requests in the following order:

$$r_2 \rightarrow r_1 \rightarrow r_3$$

1.10.2 Highest Priority Group First (HPGF)

The Highest Priority Group First (HPGF) algorithm [31] schedules data requests based on their priorities, which can be assigned based on factors such as transaction criticality, deadline tightness, or data request size. The algorithm groups request with the same priority level and services them using the SCAN disk scheduling method within each group. For example, let P_{ij} denote the priority of request r_{ij}. The HPGF algorithm can be described as follows:

Sort data requests in descending order by P_{ij}.
For each priority group, apply SCAN to schedule requests.

Example: Consider a disk with tracks numbered from 1 to 10 and data requests $R = r_1, r_2, r_3$ with track numbers $T_1 = 4$, $T_2 = 8$, and $T_3 = 2$ and priorities $P_1 = 3$, $P_2 = 1$, and $P_3 = 2$, respectively. If the disk arm is currently at track 6 and moving towards the higher-numbered tracks, the HPGF algorithm schedules the requests in the following order:

$$r\_1 \rightarrow r\_3 \rightarrow r\_2$$

1.10.3 Adaptive Earliest Deadline First (A-EDF)

Adaptive Earliest Deadline First (A-EDF) is an enhancement of the Earliest Deadline First (EDF) algorithm, which considers the history of disk accesses to predict and adapt to future disk access patterns. In the original EDF algorithm, I/O requests are prioritized based on their deadlines, with the earliest deadline request served first [60].

A-EDF enhances the EDF algorithm by considering the access history of the disk. It calculates a moving average of previous deadlines to predict the deadline of the subsequent request. This prediction is then used to adjust the scheduling of the new requests. A-EDF uses a weighted moving average to give more importance to recent deadlines, allowing it to adapt more quickly to changes in the system's behavior. The main goal of A-EDF is to improve system throughput and reduce overall missed deadlines.

Suppose there are three I/O requests, R1, R2, and R3, with deadlines D1, D2, and D3, respectively. In the EDF algorithm, the requests are scheduled according to their deadlines, i.e., R1, R2, and R3. However, in A-EDF, the scheduler also considers the disk access history. Suppose the access history suggests that requests with similar deadlines to D2 and D3 will likely be issued soon. In that case, the scheduler might adjust the scheduling order, for example, to R1, R3, and R2, to improve overall system performance.

1.10.4 Adaptive Feasible Deadline SCAN (A-FDSCAN)

Adaptive Feasible Deadline SCAN (A-FDSCAN) is an extension of the Feasible Deadline SCAN (FD-SCAN) algorithm that incorporates an adaptability mechanism [60]. FD-SCAN combines the deadline information with the SCAN algorithm, where the disk arm moves in one direction and serves requests along the way, reversing direction only when there are no more requests in the current direction.

A-FDSCAN enhances FD-SCAN by considering the current system state and the history of previous deadlines. It dynamically calculates a threshold that influences the scheduling decision. This threshold is determined by considering the moving average of prior deadlines and the current system load. The main goal of A-FDSCAN is to improve the disk scheduling performance by adaptively considering the trade-off between serving requests based on their deadlines and minimizing disk arm movements.

Suppose there are three I/O requests, R1, R2, and R3, with deadlines D1, D2, and D3, respectively, and located on tracks T1, T2, and T3. In FD-SCAN, the requests would be scheduled based on the SCAN order while considering the feasibility of meeting their deadlines. A-FDSCAN adds an adaptive component to this scheduling by adjusting the order based on a calculated threshold. Suppose the access history suggests that the calculated threshold should be reduced. In that case, the scheduler may prioritize reducing disk arm movement, potentially changing the scheduling order from R1, R2, and R3 to R1, R3, and R2, for example.

1.10.5 Dynamic I/O Scheduling for Real-Time Systems

This research presents a dynamic I/O scheduling algorithm designed for real-time systems [22]. The algorithm combines deadline and track distance information in a heuristic approach to schedule disk requests in real-time environments. The algorithm aims to minimize the number of missed deadlines by considering the system's current state and dynamically adjusting the scheduling strategy.

Suppose there are three I/O requests, R1, R2, and R3, with deadlines D1, D2, and D3, respectively, and located on tracks T1, T2, and T3. The dynamic I/O scheduling algorithm evaluates each request based on a heuristic that considers both the deadline and the distance to the request's track. This approach allows the scheduler to balance the need to meet deadlines with the need to minimize disk arm movement. For example, if R1 has the earliest deadline but is on a track much farther away from the current disk arm position than R2 and R3, the scheduler may choose to serve R2 or R3 first, depending on their deadlines and track distances. This could potentially lead to an improved overall system performance and a reduced number of missed deadlines. While the dynamic I/O scheduling algorithm was not specifically designed for real-time databases, its heuristic-based approach and consideration of system dynamics could potentially be adapted for real-time database systems.

1.10.6 Machine Learning-based Scheduling

Recent research has explored the application of machine learning techniques, such as reinforcement learning and neural networks, to optimize I/O scheduling in real-time database systems [116, 118]. These approaches aim to learn the best scheduling policy from historical data or online experiences.

1.10.6.1 Machine Learning-based I/O Scheduler for Real-time Database Systems

In the paper *Machine Learning-based I/O Scheduler for Real-time Database Systems* by Zhang et al. [118], the authors present an I/O scheduling framework that employs machine learning techniques to optimize the performance of real-time database systems. The proposed framework focuses on reinforcement learning, a type of machine learning where an agent learns to make decisions by interacting with an environment to achieve a goal.

The framework consists of three main components: State Space, Action Space, and Q-learning Algorithm. The State Space represents the system's current state, considering factors such as I/O request deadlines, disk arm position, and system load. The Action Space comprises available scheduling actions for the current state, like choosing which I/O request to serve next. Finally, the Q-learning Algorithm learns the optimal scheduling policy by iteratively updating the Q-values, representing the expected cumulative reward for each state-action pair.

Suppose there are three I/O requests, R1, R2, and R3, with deadlines D1, D2, and D3, respectively, and located on tracks T1, T2, and T3. The reinforcement learning-based I/O scheduler would consider the system's current state (e.g., the disk arm position and request deadlines) and take actions based on its learned Q-values. It may prioritize R1 because the Q-learning algorithm has learned that serving requests with the earliest deadlines usually leads to a higher cumulative reward. As the scheduler continues interacting with the environment and receiving feedback through rewards, it refines its policy to make better scheduling decisions.

The authors in [118] evaluated their proposed scheduler using simulation experiments, comparing it to traditional I/O scheduling algorithms such as FCFS, SSTF, and SCAN. The results indicated that the machine learning-based I/O scheduler outperformed the traditional algorithms in various real-time scenarios, achieving lower average response times and higher system throughput.

1.10.6.2 A Deep Reinforcement Learning-based I/O Scheduler for Real-time Database Systems

In the paper *A Deep Reinforcement Learning-based I/O Scheduler for Real-time Database Systems* by Wu et al. [116], the authors propose a deep Q-network (DQN) based model to learn an optimal I/O scheduling policy for real-time database systems. The DQN model uses a neural network to approximate the optimal action-value function, allowing the scheduler to make better decisions by considering complex relationships between I/O requests and the current system state.

The authors develop a state representation that captures the characteristics of the I/O requests, including their deadlines, arrival times, and disk track locations. The action space consists of choosing which I/O request to serve next. The deep Q-network is trained using a variant of Q-learning, incorporating techniques like experience replay and target network updating to stabilize learning.

Assume there are three I/O requests, R1, R2, and R3, with deadlines D1, D2, and D3, respectively, and located on tracks T1, T2, and T3. The DQN-based scheduler encodes the current state and feeds it into the neural network. The network then predicts the Q-values for each possible action. Suppose the Q-values indicate that serving R2 would result in the highest cumulative reward; the scheduler selects R2 to serve next. As more I/O requests are processed, the DQN continues to learn and refine its policy, adapting to the changing system dynamics.

The authors evaluated their DQN-based scheduler using simulation experiments and compared its performance to traditional I/O scheduling algorithms such as EDF, SSTF, and SCAN. The results demonstrated that the deep reinforcement learning-based I/O scheduler achieved better performance than conventional algorithms in meeting deadlines and reducing response times. In addition, the DQN-based scheduler proved to be more adaptive to various system workloads, dynamically adjusting its scheduling policy based on the current state and characteristics of the I/O requests.

1.11 Buffer Management in Real-Time Database Management Systems

Buffer management is fundamental to database management systems (DBMS), including real-time database management systems (RTDBMS). The buffer manager is responsible for managing memory buffers that temporarily store disk pages fetched by the DBMS. Therefore, buffer management's efficiency directly impacts the DBMS's performance. However, the buffer management problem becomes more complex in RTDBMS due to the additional constraint of meeting deadlines associated with real-time transactions.

The primary objective of buffer management algorithms in RTDBMS is to minimize the number of page faults while adhering to real-time constraints. A page fault occurs when a requested page is unavailable in the buffer, requiring the system to fetch the page from the disk. Disk accesses are significantly slower than memory accesses, so a high page fault rate can lead to increased response times and missed deadlines for real-time transactions. Therefore, practical buffer management algorithms must consider the deadlines and priorities of real-time transactions to ensure that the most critical pages are readily available in the buffer.

1.11.1 Deadline-Driven Page Replacement (DDPR) Algorithm

The Deadline-Driven Page Replacement (DDPR) algorithm, proposed by Abbott and Garcia-Molina [4], focuses on real-time constraints by prioritizing pages in the buffer based on their associated deadlines. When a page fault occurs, DDPR replaces the page with the earliest deadline among the pages that belong to incomplete transactions.

DDPR uses two data structures: the Buffer Table and the Deadline Table. The Buffer Table is an in-memory index that maps a page identifier to its buffer frame, whereas the Deadline Table contains entries sorted by deadlines.

To maintain the Deadline Table, DDPR updates it whenever:

1. **A transaction begins**: the deadline of the new transaction is added to the table.
2. **A transaction ends**: the deadline associated with the completed transaction is removed from the table.
3. **A page is accessed**: the deadline entry for the accessed page is updated.

When a page fault occurs, DDPR proceeds with the following steps:

1. Determine the victim page by finding the page with the earliest deadline in the Deadline Table.
2. If the victim page is dirty (i.e., modified but not yet, written to disk), issue a write request to save the changes to disk.
3. Issue a read request to fetch the requested page from disk.
4. Update the Buffer Table and Deadline Table to reflect the new state.

Although DDPR can improve the likelihood of meeting real-time constraints by prioritizing pages with urgent deadlines, it may suffer from high page fault rates, mainly when transactions with similar deadlines compete for buffer space. This issue can be mitigated by incorporating other factors, such as page access frequencies, into the replacement policy.

1.11.2 Priority-Driven Buffer Management (PDBM) Algorithm

The Priority-Driven Buffer Management (PDBM) algorithm, proposed by Kamath et al. [45], combines deadline-driven and LRU page replacement strategies. PDBM divides the buffer into two segments: one for real-time transactions and another for non-real-time transactions.

PDBM uses two data structures to manage the buffer: the Real-Time Segment (RTS) Table and the Non-Real-Time Segment (NRTS) Table. The RTS Table contains buffer frame entries sorted by transaction deadlines, while the NRTS Table maintains buffer frame entries following an LRU order.

The steps in PDBM are as follows:

1. When a page fault occurs, determine whether the request belongs to a real-time or non-real-time transaction.
2. If the request is for a real-time transaction, use the RTS Table to find the page with the earliest deadline among the real-time pages in the buffer and mark it as the victim page for a replacement.
3. If the request is for a non-real-time transaction, use the NRTS Table to find the least recently used non-real-time page in the buffer and mark it as the victim page for a replacement.
4. If the victim page is dirty, issue a write request to save the changes to disk.
5. Issue a read request to fetch the requested page from disk.
6. Update the RTS Table and NRTS Table to reflect the new state.

By combining deadline-driven and LRU-based strategies, PDBM aims to balance the performance requirements of both real-time and non-real-time transactions while ensuring that real-time deadlines are met. However, PDBM uses a fixed-size buffer segment for real-time transactions, which may not be optimal under varying system workloads.

1.11.3 Adaptive Real-Time Buffer Management (ARTBM) Algorithm

The Adaptive Real-Time Buffer Management (ARTBM) algorithm, proposed by Huang et al. [40], addresses the limitations of PDBM by dynamically adjusting the size of the real-time buffer segment according to system workload and transaction deadlines. ARTBM also combines deadline-driven and LRU page replacement strategies.

ARTBM maintains the same RTS Table and NRTS Table as PDBM, but it also uses a global table called the Free Frame Pool (FFP). The FFP contains buffer frames not currently allocated to the RTS or NRTS segments.

When a page fault occurs, ARTBM follows these steps:

1. Determine if the request belongs to a real-time or non-real-time transaction.
2. If the request is for a real-time transaction and there is an available frame in the FFP, allocate it to the RTS segment. Otherwise, use the RTS Table to find the page with the earliest deadline among the real-time pages in the buffer and mark it as the victim page for a replacement.
3. If the request is for a non-real-time transaction, use the NRTS Table to find the least recently used non-real-time page in the buffer and mark it as the victim page for a replacement. If there is an available frame in the FFP, allocate it to the NRTS segment.

4. If the victim page is dirty, issue a written request to save the changes to disk.
5. Issue a read request to fetch the requested page from disk.
6. Update the RTS Table, NRTS Table, and FFP to reflect the new state.

By dynamically adjusting the size of the real-time buffer segment based on the system's state, ARTBM ensures more efficient utilization of memory resources and improves the overall performance of the RTDBMS.

1.11.3.1 Prediction-Based Buffer Management (PBBM) Algorithm: Detailed Description

The Prediction-Based Buffer Management (PBBM) algorithm, proposed by Zhu and Chiueh [120], relies on access pattern predictions to optimize buffer management. PBBM identifies frequently accessed pages by analyzing their access patterns and keeps these pages in the buffer to minimize page faults.

PBBM consists of three main components: the Pattern Detector, the Pattern Predictor, and the Buffer Manager. The Pattern Detector analyzes the access history of each page to identify recurring patterns. The Pattern Predictor uses the detected patterns to forecast future page accesses. Finally, the Buffer Manager replaces pages in the buffer based on the predictions provided by the Pattern Predictor.

When a page fault occurs, PBBM follows these steps:

1. Check the Pattern Predictor's forecasts to determine which pages are expected to be accessed in the near future.
2. If the requested page is predicted to be accessed frequently, replace a page in the buffer that is not predicted to be accessed in the near future, marking it as the victim page for a replacement.
3. If the requested page is not predicted to be accessed frequently, replace the least recently used page in the buffer, marking it as the victim page for a replacement.
4. If the victim page is dirty, issue a written request to save the changes to disk.
5. Issue a read request to fetch the requested page from disk.
6. Update the access history and re-evaluate the access patterns as necessary.

Using access pattern predictions, PBBM can make informed decisions on which pages should be kept in the buffer and which should be replaced. As a result, this approach minimizes page faults and improves the system's overall performance.

1.12 Related Developments

Real-time database systems are a dynamic and rapidly developing area in the field of computer science. The need for real-time access to data has increased across various domains, including telecommunications, financial services, healthcare, and many others. As a result, several research areas and recent developments have emerged to address the challenges and needs of real-time database systems. In this section, we show few examples of related developments to real-time database systems.

1.12.1 Main-Memory Databases

In the context of real-time database systems, main memory databases (MMDBs) have been increasingly significant in the recent past. The primary objective of these databases is to maintain high-speed data processing while dealing with the volume of modern data transactions. As opposed to traditional disk-based databases, MMDBs store all data in the primary memory (RAM), bypassing the time-consuming disk I/O operations and thus fulfilling the stringent timing requirements of real-time systems.

Main memory databases primarily leverage the high-speed access of RAM to provide swift data transaction. The fundamental premise is to eliminate the bottleneck of disk I/O, which has been a crucial issue in traditional databases. MMDBs are essential for applications with stringent time constraints such as financial trading systems, telecommunications, real-time analytics, and high-speed online transaction processing (OLTP). In essence, MMDBs are designed to take advantage of the decreasing cost of RAM, the growing need for real-time data access, and the continuing advancements in multi-core and multi-processor technology.

The architecture of an MMDB is designed to optimize memory utilization and exploit the benefits of high-speed data access. Unlike disk-based databases, which employ a page-oriented approach, MMDBs use structures like T-trees, B+ trees, or hash indexes for data storage and retrieval, to provide quick and direct access to memory locations. The concurrency control mechanisms are specifically designed to manage simultaneous data access and modifications, ensuring data consistency. Recovery mechanisms are also established to handle system failures, with strategies such as shadow paging and checkpointing, which ensure data durability and reliability, even when entirely residing in volatile memory.

The most significant advantage of MMDBs is their high performance in data processing. By eliminating the disk I/O operations, they can execute transactions several times faster than traditional databases. Additionally, they can support real-time applications with stringent time requirements, providing almost instantaneous response times. Despite their benefits, MMDBs are not without their challenges. The primary constraint is the volatile nature of RAM. Power failures can lead to data loss, mitigated only by backup and recovery mechanisms. Cost is another factor, as even though memory prices are declining, RAM is still considerably more expensive than disk storage. Additionally, existing database systems might require significant modifications to adapt to an MMDB system.

1.12.2 Real-Time Data Analytics

In an era characterized by high-speed digital transformation, the capability to analyze and interpret data instantaneously has become critical. Real-time data analytics, a technology that provides immediate processing and analysis of data, is significantly influencing the design and functionality of real-time database systems. This chapter delves into the role of real-time data analytics, its mechanisms, and how it shapes the evolution of real-time database systems.

Real-time data analytics pertains to the immediate processing and analysis of data as it is created and ingested into the system. It endeavors to deliver insights and extrapolate patterns with minimal latency, often within milliseconds to a few seconds. Such quick turnaround times facilitate immediate decision-making and responses, providing a competitive edge in fields like finance, health care, e-commerce, and logistics. Diverging from the traditional batch-processing model, real-time analytics processes data in a continuous stream as it is generated. This approach is powered by real-time stream processing technologies such as Apache Kafka, Apache Flink, and Apache Storm. These technologies are adept at processing and analyzing live data streams, thus empowering real-time database systems to generate instantaneous insights and actionable intelligence.

"Streaming data" or "real-time data" is dynamic data continuously generated from various sources like sensors, cameras, social media feeds, and cameras. Examples of real-time data are e-commerce purchases, geo-location tracking, server activity, health data, website activity, weather events, and utility service usage. When companies can process all that data as it's coming in, they can near-instantaneously gain insight and understand exactly what's going on with their customers or internal business processes, but data on its own doesn't lead to business-building breakthroughs.

Real-time (streaming) analytics make sense of all the real-time data that flows into a company. When businesses can analyze data in real-time, they can generate insights while the data is in the stream, instead of storing and analyzing it in batches. Traditionally, data analysis happens once the data has been captured and stored. Then any business insights are pushed out from storage. But real-time data analysis replaces that process, helping companies make more accurate decisions and take action significantly faster.

Real-time data analytics is a technique that analyzes data as it happens. It takes advantage of the fact that, for many applications, traditional batch analytics tools are actually working in the wrong direction – not just by analyzing data at a later time, but by actually waiting for data to arrive. That data gap can cause lags in decision-making that can cost companies time, money, and energy.

Streaming data is almost always more profitable data. Companies know that most data has a short shelf life, so the faster they can turn information into insight, the more valuable all that data will be.

Companies can use real-time data analytics to:

- Predict customer behaviors.
- Solve the technical problems associated with typical data batching processing.

- Make more efficient Decision-Making.
- Scale faster.
- Help to provide anomaly detection.
- Make better business decisions.
- Act proactively to maximize customer satisfaction.
- Increase operational efficiency and reaction time.
- Create more intelligent products and services.
- Improve and automate business processes.

1.12.3 Time-Series Databases

Time-series databases (TSDBs) have emerged as a critical component in the sphere of real-time database systems. As organizations deal with an ever-growing volume of time-stamped data, the utility of databases specifically designed to handle this type of data has become increasingly evident. This chapter provides an in-depth understanding of time-series databases, their importance, and their influence on real-time database systems.

A time-series database is a database management system optimized for handling time-stamped or time-series data. Time-series data is a sequence of data points collected over time, typically consisting of successive measurements made over a time interval. Examples of time-series data include stock prices, weather data, sensor data, and server metrics.

Time-series databases are designed to efficiently collect, store efficiently, and query time-series data with high write and query speeds. They handle the time aspect of data in a more explicit and optimized way compared to traditional databases. Examples of time-series databases include InfluxDB, OpenTSDB, and TimescaleDB.

The integration of time-series databases into real-time database systems yields several transformative effects:

- **High-Performance Data Analysis**: Time-series databases are specifically optimized for high-speed data writes. This is essential for real-time database systems, which often need to handle a substantial influx of real-time data.
- **Efficient Data Querying**: TSDBs are designed to allow efficient querying of time-series data. This efficiency makes them well-suited to real-time database systems, where users often need to retrieve and analyze historical time-series data in real time.
- **Scalability**: TSDBs are typically built to be scalable, making them suitable for real-time database systems that need to handle large volumes of data.
- **Data Compression**: TSDBs can compress time-series data, saving storage space while still allowing efficient querying. This feature is critical in real-time database systems, where large volumes of data are generated continuously.

Despite the evident benefits, the incorporation of time-series databases into real-time database systems presents several challenges:

- **Complexity of Time-Series Data**: Time-series data can be complex and multi-dimensional. Managing and extracting useful information from this data can be a challenging task.
- **Data Retention and Storage**: Given that time-series databases deal with data that is continuously generated, determining how long to store data, when to archive it, and when to discard it are crucial considerations.
- **Data Privacy and Security**: As with any database system, ensuring data privacy and security is a paramount concern for time-series databases.

1.12.4 NoSQL Databases

With an exponential increase in data volume and variety, traditional SQL databases have often struggled to meet the evolving requirements of real-time database systems. This has led to the emergence of NoSQL databases, which provide a flexible, scalable, and efficient solution for managing complex data in real time. This chapter aims to explore the nature of NoSQL databases, their significance, and their transformative impact on real-time database systems.

NoSQL, which stands for "Not Only SQL," is a type of database that provides a mechanism for storage and retrieval of data modeled in means other than the tabular relations used in relational databases. NoSQL databases are particularly useful for handling unstructured, distributed, and large volumes of data. They are categorized into four main types: document databases, key-value databases, wide-column databases, and graph databases. NoSQL databases, such as MongoDB, Cassandra, and Couchbase, offer scalability, flexibility, and high performance, making them well-suited for real-time database systems.

The integration of NoSQL databases into real-time database systems brings transformative changes:

- **Flexible Data Models**: Unlike SQL databases, which require a predefined schema, NoSQL databases are schema-less. This allows for the storage of complex and heterogeneous data, which is often the case in real-time database systems.
- **High Scalability**: NoSQL databases are designed to scale out by distributing the data across many servers. This is critical for real-time database systems, which often deal with large volumes of incoming data.
- **High Performance**: NoSQL databases are optimized for specific data models (such as key-value pairs or graphs), which can lead to better performance when dealing with large datasets in real-time.

Despite their advantages, the incorporation of NoSQL databases into real-time database systems presents several challenges:

- **Complexity**: NoSQL databases can be complex to implement and manage due to their distributed nature. Managing data consistency across distributed systems can be particularly challenging.

- **Security**: While NoSQL databases have made strides in security features, they still generally lag behind SQL databases in this regard. As real-time database systems often handle sensitive data, this can be a significant concern.

However, the NoSQL field is advancing rapidly, with continuous improvements being made in areas such as security, data consistency, and management tools. Future directions will likely focus on further enhancements in these areas and in developing more efficient data processing techniques.

Chapter 2
Experimental Real-Time Databases

Since the early '90s, researchers have proposed numerous prototypes to study the difficulties that arise in real-time databases. In this chapter, we shall review several experimental implementations that depict the progress made in real-time databases and whose development spans the last three decades. The first two, **STRIP** and **BeeHive**, are significant because they set up the pathway for further advancements.

Experimental real-time database systems refer to database management systems (DBMS) that are developed and implemented for research purposes to explore and evaluate novel techniques, algorithms, and approaches in handling real-time data. These systems are not typically intended for production environments but serve as testbeds for researchers and developers to investigate and validate new ideas, algorithms, and architectures. Experimental real-time database systems are designed to address the unique challenges posed by real-time applications, which require timely data processing, predictable response times, and adherence to strict timing constraints. These systems aim to explore innovative solutions to achieve high performance, determinism, and predictability in managing and processing real-time data.

The primary objective of experimental real-time database systems is to advance the understanding and development of real-time data management techniques. They serve as platforms for researchers and developers to explore innovative ideas, validate theoretical concepts, and identify potential areas for improvement in real-time data processing. By utilizing experimental real-time database systems, researchers and developers can gain insights into the performance characteristics, limitations, and trade-offs of different approaches in handling real-time data. The knowledge gained from such experiments can guide the design and development of more efficient and effective real-time database systems for various applications and domains.

This chapter explores various experimental academic real-time database systems and their approaches to handling real-time requirements. It provides an overview of these systems, including their models, architectures, and unique characteristics.

© The Author(s), under exclusive license to Springer Nature Switzerland AG 2024
P. Mejia Alvarez et al., *Real-Time Database Systems*, SpringerBriefs in Computer Science,
https://doi.org/10.1007/978-3-031-44230-8_2

2.1 STRIP

STRIP (Stanford Real-time Information Processor) [6, 19] is a soft real-time main memory database for heterogeneous environments developed at Stanford between 1994 and 1996. It had special facilities for importing and exporting data and handling derived data. STRIP was developed to run on standard Posix Unix and intended to support soft timing constraints, high performance, and high availability and to allow sharing of data with other components in a bigger system. This capability can be seen in the process architecture of STRIP shown in figure 2.1.

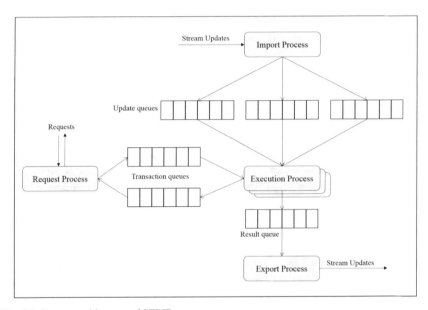

Fig. 2.1 Process architecture of STRIP.

STRIP was explicitly designed to share data with other systems, both traditional database systems and other entities, such as real-time market feeds. The first design goal was to isolate the database user, as much as possible, from the knowledge of where data originates or is sent. The second was to interface with as many different types of systems as possible, including non-database systems.

2.1.1 STRIP Real-Time Scheduling

Tasks in STRIP are the units of scheduling. A task may contain zero or more transactions but cannot span task boundaries. Associated with each task in STRIP is a value function, as shown in Figure 2.2, which indicates how valuable it is to the system to complete the task at a particular point in time. The release time, R, determines how long the database system holds a task before it can be scheduled. After being released, its value function is composed of three linear segments connecting the points A,B,C, and D. Points B, C, and D do not have to have positive value or have the relative values shown in Figure 2.2. Further, the value of the function stays at its value at D for all time beyond D.

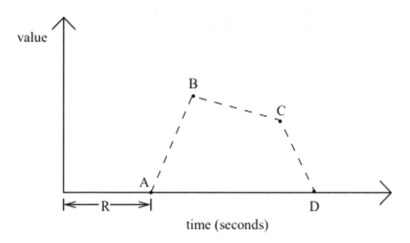

Fig. 2.2 Specification of a value function in STRIP.

STRIP provides the following choices for task scheduling:

1. First in First Out (FIFO) - Tasks are scheduled in the order that they are released.
2. Earliest Deadline First (EDF) - The released task with the nearest deadline is scheduled first (the deadline of a task is assumed to be the time it reaches point C). Ties are resolved in FIFO order.
3. Highest Value first (HV) - The released task with the greatest maximum value is scheduled first. Ties are resolved with FIFO.
4. Highest value density first (VD) - The released task with the largest ratio of value at completion to time to completion is scheduled next. Ties are resolved with FIFO. This algorithm requires an estimate of the time to completion.

STRIP only supports the scheduling of tasks. Although user tasks can contain multiple transactions, some work in the system is performed outside of user tasks. For instance, data import and export rule actions occur in particular system tasks. The application can specify value functions for these tasks as described later in this chapter. Hence a user cannot select an end-to-end value function for a series of actions such as: importing a record, recomputing everything it derives, export the newly derived values. Instead, the global value function must be decomposed into value functions for each of the three component actions.

2.1.2 Data Sharing Architecture

STRIP's underlying data-sharing model is the publish/subscribe model. Data sources publish tables which are then available by subscription to other system components. The subscriber receives a real-time stream of information that allows it to maintain a current copy of the table as it changes at the source. The format of the streams is discussed in the next section. To isolate a naive user from publication and subscription details, STRIP logically divides all of the sharing functionality into four levels, shown in Figure 2.3. The remote level is implemented on the publisher's machine, but the other three levels are implemented within STRIP. Let us explore each level in turn.

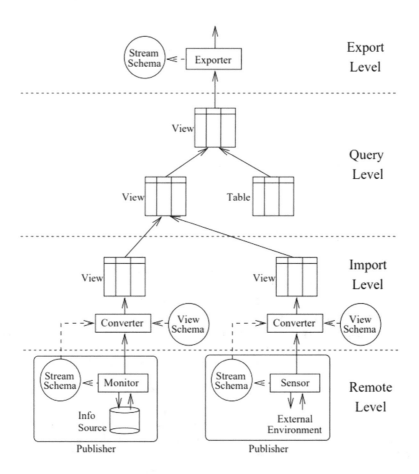

Fig. 2.3 System Architecture of STRIP.

1. **Remote Level**: The remote level is concerned with capturing data changes in remote data sources and then translating them into a stream format that can be understood by the import level (introduced next). The remote level is target-specific; it may be based on relational systems, chronicles (append-only tables), legacy systems, or conventional files. In the cases where the remote data is stored (e.g., in a file system or a database system), it is the monitor's job to extract the information using the appropriate mechanisms.

2. **Import Level**: The import level converts remote data streams into local views. This conversion presents the query level with a single paradigm for all imported data regardless of its original format. The format of the local view does not have to match that of the stream it is derived from. The mapping is described in the view schema. The views defined in this level are limited, however, in that they can be derived from only one stream (although one stream can generate many views). Views that combine data from different streams must be defined at the query level. The syntax for the import view definition is presented later in the chapter.

3. **Query Level**: The query level contains the functionality typically associated with a relational database system. Views and tables can be defined, modified, and queried. Import views appear in the query level as read-only tables to the application code. If the underlying data source has active rules, they can extract the deltas without requiring changes to the application code.

4. **Export Level**: The external level allows applications to define the views exported from STRIP. It then handles the details of the stream protocol to act as a data publisher.

2.1.3 Streams Support

Streams provide the underlying support for the publish/subscribe model presented to the user of STRIP. The stream format is very flexible, allowing the source to send incremental changes to its table or complete refreshes. This and other options are described below. The one restriction on the model is that streams only support unidirectional flow. The subscribers cannot pose queries to the publishers through it. However, if a query needs to be answered, the subscriber can contact the publisher directly through its normal query interface. This decision simplifies the protocol design without reducing the system's functionality. The largest unit of information transferred over a stream is an update. An update can be one of four types:

1. A physical delta update contains the tuples inserted into, deleted from, and updated in the remote table.
2. A logical delta update contains SQL statements that have been performed on the remote table to change it.
3. A snapshot update contains the entire set of tuples in the remote table. a control update contains format or handshake information.

2.1.4 View Definition

This section describes the view definition constructs provided by STRIP. They are based on SQL/12, but extend the standard to support import and export views as well as real-time constraints on update transmission. The extensions are outlined below.

```
create import view import-view-name
from stream-name
as select [all distinct] column-comma-list
where cond-exp
group by column-ref-commalist
having cond-exp
[ with ownership ]
[ schedule fusing value function value-function immediately]
```

Fig. 2.4 Data import SQL statements.

1. **Import Views**: The syntax of the import view definition is shown in Figure 2.4. The stream named $stream - name$ defines the logical table upon which the view is defined. Recall from the previous section that import views can be defined on only one import stream. Thus import views are defined by single table queries over the "table" published by a stream. Since it is over only one table, the query cannot contain joins (including $self - joins$); it is limited to selection, projection, and aggregation. The new view will be named $import - view - name$, and will contain the columns defined in $column - comma - list$.

2. **Export Views and Tables**:
   The syntax for exporting data from STRIP is shown in Figure 2.5. The create export command creates and publishes a new stream. The table or view to be exported is specified by the send clause. The statement can specify an optional list of destination addresses representing initial subscribers. This list can also be modified later using the add subscribers and delete subscribers statements shown in Figure 2.6. When a new subscriber is added for a stream, either at stream creation or after using the add subscribers statement, a snapshot of the current state of $table - view - name$ is sent. After that, export timing is determined by the when clause, which specifies when updates for the supported table or view should be marked for export to subscribers. When data is marked for exportation, a task is created to send the data and scheduled according to the value function specified in the export statement. STRIP provides three options for the when clause to specify when rows should be marked for exportation. The first is when directed, which leaves the decision entirely in the hands of the application programmer. STRIP will not export any data until the application executes the flush export stream statement shown in Figure 2.6. The user can create sophisticated export schemes by embedding the flush export stream statement into the action of rules.

3. **View Mapping**: The three levels present within STRIP (import, query and, export) are conceptually defined by the application designer as tables and views. We call the collection of these de

nitions the conceptual schema. Because the conceptual schema does not specify which views are to be materialized and because the view hierarchy is designed for clarity rather than efficiency, a straightforward implementation of the conceptual schema may result in poor performance. Rather than forcing system designers to manually tune the system (choosing which views to materialize, redefining views in more efficient ways), STRIP should harness usage information provided both by the designers and by run-time statistics to perform the transformation automatically.

```
create export export-stream-name
send table-view-name
[to inet-address-list]
when f directed j changed j older than age using timestamp-colg
updates are f [strictly] physical j [strictly] logical j snapshots g
[inserts are fcomplete j partialg]
[deletes are fcomplete j partialg]
[modifies are fcomplete j partialg [after image only]]
[with ownership]
[value function value-function ]
inet-address-list ::= inet-address [inet-address-list]
inet-address ::= fip-address j machine-nameg : port-number
```

Fig. 2.5 Data export SQL statements.

```
add subscribers inet-address-list
for stream export-stream-name
delete subscribers inet-address-list
from stream export-stream-name
push export stream export-stream-name
where cond-exp
```

Fig. 2.6 Additional SQL statement for export streams.

2.2 BeeHive Real-Time Database

BeeHive resulted from collaborative work between the University of Virginia and Hoseo University between 1997 and 2007 [106]. This system was used to investigate the impact of data validity intervals on the performance of real-time databases. Unfortunately, most of the previous prototypes discussed so far only consider the deadlines of the transactions.

The BeeHive system that is currently being defined has many innovative components including:

- Real-time database support based on a new notion of *data deadlines* rather than just transaction deadlines.
- Parallel and real-time recovery based on the semantics of data and system operational mode (e.g., crisis mode).
- Use of reactive information and a specification language to support adaptive fault tolerance real-time performance and security.
- The idea of security rules embedded into objects together with the ability for these rules to utilize profiles of various types
- Composable fault-tolerant objects that synergistically operate with the transaction properties of databases and with real-time logging and recovery
- A new architecture and model of interaction between multimedia and transaction processing.
- A uniform task model for simultaneously supporting hard real-time control tasks and end-to-end multimedia processing and
- New real-time QoS scheduling resource management and renegotiation algorithms.

2.2.1 Beehive Architecture

The BeeHive project builds upon these results and combines them into a novel design for a global virtual database.

BeeHive consists of three components:

- BeeHive database server
- Transaction thread pool
- BeeKeeper resource manager

The arrangement of these three elements is depicted in Figure 2.7.

The BeeKeeper acts as the resource manager process. The service mapper acts as a transaction generator. The admission controller receives transactions from the mapper and determines if BeeHive has enough CPU and I/O resources. Once the transaction is admitted, the real-time scheduler assigns a priority based on some policy. Finally, the object manager generates a BeeHive object that encapsulates the transaction and uses an RPC to connect to the BeeHive database server. The architecture of the BeeHive database server is shown in figure 2.8. The listener thread receives RPC connections from the BeeKeeper and gets a transaction thread from a pool to service each connecting client. The transaction thread serves the received RPC, which represents a transaction. The transaction process consists of executing

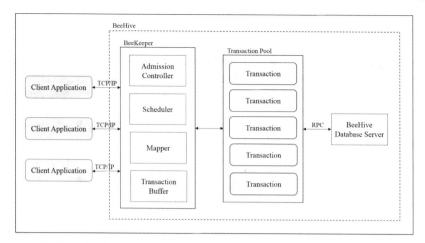

Fig. 2.7 BeeHive Architecture.

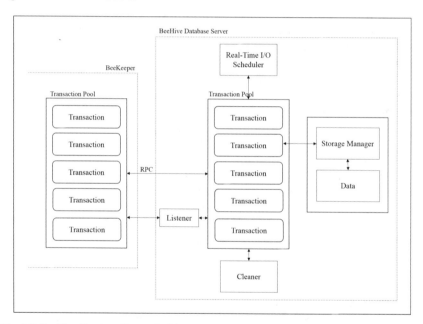

Fig. 2.8 BeeHive Database Server Architecture.

the operations in the SHORE server. SHORE is a database system developed at the University of Wisconsin that provides ACID transactions, concurrency control, and disk I/O management.

The system manages two types of transactions: user transactions and sensor transactions. Sensor transactions update the temporal data frequently, and user transaction reads this data along with other non-temporal data. Temporal data, as discussed previously, includes an absolute data validity interval (AVI).

2.2.2 Beehive Real-Time Scheduling

The BeeHive project evaluates three real-time scheduling policies: Earliest Deadline First (EDF), Earliest Data-Deadline First (EDDF), and Earliest Deadline First with Data Validity Check (EDF-DC). Notice that EDDF and EDF-DC are data-deadline cognizant scheduling policies.

In [106], admission control is performed in two steps. Firstly, it calculates the expected CPU utilization and the I/O utilization:

$$U(CPU) = \left(\sum_{i=1}^{n} \frac{CPUTime(T_i)}{DL(T_i) - t} + \frac{CPUTime(T)}{DL(T) - t} \right) * 100 \qquad (2.1)$$

$$U(IO) = \left(\sum_{i=1}^{n} \frac{IOTime(T_i)}{DL(T_i) - t} + \frac{IOTime(T)}{DL(T) - t} \right) * 100 \qquad (2.2)$$

where T_i is each of the transactions currently in the system, and T is the incoming transaction. $IOTime(T_i)$ and $CPUTime(T_i)$ are pre-analyzed. In each experiment, thresholds for each of these utilizations are defined. If the utilizations are higher than the thresholds at this step, then the transaction T is rejected.

The second step in the admission control process is performed when the transaction is taken for execution, and it consists in checking for the system response time. The system response time should be shorter than the transaction's slack time, that is:

$$DL(T) - t > c * \frac{\sum_{i=1}^{n} ERT(T_i)}{n} \qquad (2.3)$$

where $DL(T)$ is the deadline of the new transaction T, $ERT(T_i)$ is the execution response time of transaction T_i and c is a constant. If the inequality holds, then the transaction is executed.

The experiments presented in [106] vary transaction execution times, relative deadlines (i.e., slack factors), and scheduling policy. Experiments with and without the admission controller are also performed. The results indicated that data-deadline cognizant scheduling policies are valuable when the data validity intervals are shorter than transaction deadlines, especially when the system load is in the medium range. However, when the system is overloaded, admission control makes a more significant difference than the scheduling policy. This improvement is observed more clearly when the transaction deadlines are shorter than the data validity intervals.

One of the drawbacks of BeeHive is that transaction execution times should be determined offline for admission control. This approach is practical only when the transactions and their arrival and data access patterns are known in advance [48], which is only sometimes the case.

2.2.3 General Beehive Design

BeeHive is an application-focused global virtual database system. BeeHive's emphasis is on sensor data, the use of time-valid data level of support for adaptive fault tolerance, support for real-time databases, security, and the unique features that deal with crisis mode operation. Parts of the system can run on fixed secure hosts, and other parts can be more dynamic such as mobile computers or general processors on the Internet. The BeeHive design is composed of native BeeHive sites and legacy sites ported to BeeHive and interfaces to legacy systems outside of BeeHive. The native BeeHive sites comprise a federated distributed database model that implements a temporal data model time-cognizant database and QoS protocols, a specification model, a mapping from this specification to four APIs, the OS network, fault tolerance, and security APIs and underlying novel object support. Any practical application will include legacy databases. BeeHive permits porting these databases into the BeeHive virtual system by a combination of wrappers and changes to the underlying software of these systems. It is essential to mention that BeeHive, while application focussed, is not isolated.

BeeHive can interact with other virtual global databases, Web browsers or individual non-application-specific databases via BeeHive wrappers. BeeHive will access these databases via downloaded Java applets that include standard SQL commands. In many situations, not only information must be identified and collected, but it must be analyzed. This analysis should be permitted to use the vast computer processing infrastructure that exists. For example, BeeHive will have a wrapper that can utilize a distributed computing environment, such as the Legion system, to provide significant processing power when needed.

2.2.4 Native BeeHive Design

The basic design of a native BeeHive site is depicted in Figure 2.8. At the application level users can submit transactions, analysis programs, general programs, and access audio and video data. For each activity, the user has a standard specification interface for real-time QoS, fault tolerance, and security. At the application level, these requirements are specified at a high-level manner. For example, a user might select a deadline, full-quality QoS display, a primary-backup fault tolerance requirement, and a confidentiality level of security. For transactions, users operate with an object-oriented database invoking methods on the data. The data model includes timestamped data and data with validity intervals, as is needed for sensor data. As transactions or other programs access objects, those objects become active, and a mapping occurs between the high-level requirements specification and the object API via the mapping module. This mapping module is primarily concerned with the interface to object wrappers and with end-to-end issues. A novel aspect of our work is that each object has semantic information also called reactive information, because it is information about the object itself. Associated with it, it makes it possible to simultaneously satisfy the requirements of time, QoS, fault tolerance, and security adaptively. For example, the information might include rules or policies and the action to take when the underlying system cannot guarantee the deadline or level of fault tolerance requested. This semantic information also includes code that makes calls to the resource management subsystem to satisfy or negotiate the resource requirements. The resource management subsystem further translates the requirements into resource-specific APIs, such as the APIs for the OS, the network, the fault tolerance support mechanisms, and the security subsystem. For example, given that a user has invoked a method on an object with a deadline and primary-backup requirement, the semantic information associated with the object makes a call to the resource manager requesting this service. The resource manager determines if it can allocate the primary and backup to execute the method before its deadline and inform the OS via the OS API of the module's priority and resource needs. In terms of this design, the main tasks to be undertaken include the full development of the high-level specification, including how these requirements interact with each other, the implementation of real-time object-oriented database support, the design, and implementation of our semantics-enhanced objects the design and implementation of the object-oriented wrappers, the mapping module's development, and the resource management, fault tolerance, and security subsystems.

2.3 RTSORAC: A Real-Time Object-Oriented Database Model

Real-Time Systems Object-Relational Active Database (RTSORAC) is a real-time object-oriented database model designed to handle the unique requirements of real-time applications. RTSORAC integrates the benefits of real-time systems, object-oriented modeling, and active databases [92]. This section discusses the fundamental concepts of RTSORAC, its applications, and a comparison with other real-time database management systems (RTDBMS).

2.3.1 RTSORAC Model

RTSORAC extends the traditional object-oriented database model with real-time features like deadlines, temporal consistency, and priority-based scheduling. It also incorporates active rules to handle real-time events and constraints. The main components of RTSORAC are real-time objects, real-time transactions, and active rules [92].

- **Real-Time Objects**: Real-Time objects in RTSORAC are instances of real-time classes, encapsulating data and behavior. Each real-time object has associated attributes, methods, and timing constraints. A real-time object is defined as follows:

$$RTObject = \langle OID, Attributes, Methods, RTConstraints \rangle \qquad (2.4)$$

where OID is the object identifier, $Attributes$ are object attributes, $Methods$ are object methods, and $RTConstraints$ are real-time constraints, such as deadlines and minimum inter-arrival times [104].

- **Real-Time Transactions**: RTSORAC defines real-time transactions as a set of operations performed on real-time objects. Real-time transactions must adhere to timing constraints, such as deadlines and temporal consistency requirements. A real-time transaction is defined as:

$$RTTransaction = \langle TID, Operations, RTConstraints \rangle \qquad (2.5)$$

where TID is the transaction identifier, $Operations$ are transaction operations, and $RTConstraints$ are real-time constraints, such as execution time and deadline [97].

- **Active Rules**: Active rules in RTSORAC are responsible for triggering actions based on specific events and conditions. They help maintain real-time constraints and ensure data consistency. An active rule is defined as:

$$ActiveRule = \langle RID, Event, Condition, Action \rangle \qquad (2.6)$$

where RID is the rule identifier, $Event$ is the triggering event, $Condition$ is the rule condition, and $Action$ is the rule action. Active rules enable RTSORAC to support event-driven systems and react to dynamic changes in the environment [75].

- **Concurrency Control**: Concurrency control is a critical aspect of any real-time database system. RTSORAC employs a priority-based concurrency control mechanism that ensures the timely execution of real-time transactions while maintaining data consistency. The priority assignment is based on the urgency of the transaction, considering its deadline and criticality [78].

- **Data Consistency and Integrity**: Maintaining data consistency and integrity is a crucial aspect of database management in RTSORAC. Real-time scheduling algorithms are used to ensure that transactions are executed in an order that maintains the consistency and integrity of the data, even in the presence of timing constraints. This involves prioritizing transactions based on their deadlines and ensuring that any dependencies between transactions are respected during scheduling.

- **Recovery and Fault Tolerance**: In real-time systems, failures can lead to missed deadlines and incorrect system behavior. RTSORAC incorporates real-time scheduling algorithms with recovery and fault tolerance mechanisms, such as checkpointing and logging, to ensure that the system can recover from failures and continue to operate correctly. By considering the timing constraints of transactions during recovery and fault tolerance, RTSORAC can minimize the impact of failures on system performance and guarantee the temporal consistency of the data.

2.3.2 Real-time Scheduling Characteristics in RTSORAC

RTSORAC employs a priority-based scheduling algorithm to manage the execution of real-time transactions. The scheduler considers factors such as deadlines, transaction priorities, and resource availability to make scheduling decisions [97]. This approach ensures that high-priority transactions are executed promptly and reduces the likelihood of deadline misses. The Earliest Deadline First (EDF) and Rate Monotonic (RM) [64] scheduling algorithms are examples of priority-based scheduling algorithms that can be used in RTSORAC.

The integration of real-time scheduling algorithms with database management in RTSORAC is essential to ensure that tasks are executed within their deadlines while maintaining the consistency and integrity of the data. By considering the timing constraints of transactions during transaction management, concurrency control, data consistency and integrity, and recovery and fault tolerance, RTSORAC can provide an effective and efficient solution for real-time database systems.

Real-time scheduling plays a crucial role in RTSORAC, as it determines the order in which tasks are executed to meet their deadlines and ensure temporal consistency. In this subsection, we describe in detail the key characteristics of real-time scheduling in RTSORAC.

1. **Timeliness**: In real-time systems, tasks have strict timing constraints that must be met to ensure correct system behavior. RTSORAC employs real-time scheduling algorithms that prioritize tasks based on their deadlines or periods to ensure that the most time-critical tasks are executed first. This timeliness characteristic is essential for maintaining the temporal consistency of the data and guaranteeing the correct operation of real-time applications.

2. **Determinism**: Determinism is the property that ensures a task will always complete within a predictable amount of time. Real-time scheduling in RTSORAC must exhibit determinism, as any uncertainty in task completion times can lead to missed deadlines and incorrect system behavior. By employing scheduling algorithms and resource management techniques that guarantee predictable task execution times, RTSORAC can maintain determinism in real-time systems.

3. **Predictability**: Predictability is the ability to estimate the completion time of a task before its execution. For example, in RTSORAC, real-time scheduling algorithms must provide predictability to enable the system to determine whether a task can meet its deadline before it starts execution. This characteristic allows the system to make informed decisions about task scheduling and resource allocation, ensuring that deadlines are met, and resources are used efficiently.

4. **Resource Management**: Resource management is the process of allocating and deallocating resources, such as CPU time, memory, and I/O devices, to tasks in a real-time system. In RTSORAC, real-time scheduling algorithms must consider resource management to ensure that tasks have the resources they need to execute within their deadlines. By managing resources effectively, RTSORAC can minimize resource contention and maximize system throughput.

5. **Adaptability**: Real-time systems often operate in dynamic environments where task characteristics, such as execution times and deadlines, may change during runtime. Therefore, RTSORAC's real-time scheduling algorithms must adapt to these changes and re-schedule tasks accordingly to ensure that deadlines are met, and system performance is maintained.

6. **Fault Tolerance**: Fault tolerance is the ability of a system to continue operating correctly in the presence of failures. For example, in RTSORAC, real-time scheduling algorithms must be fault-tolerant, as any failure in task execution can lead to missed deadlines and incorrect system behavior. By incorporating fault-tolerance techniques, such as redundancy, error detection, and recovery mechanisms, RTSORAC can ensure the correct operation of real-time systems in the face of failures.

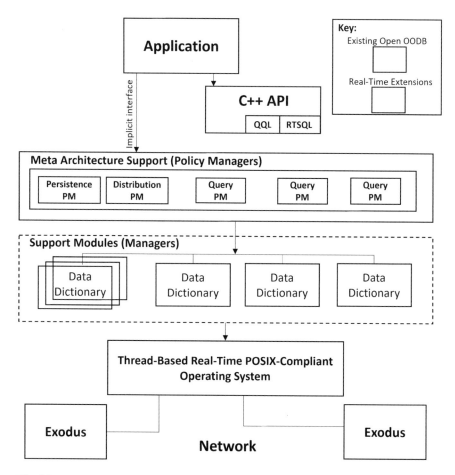

Fig. 2.9 RTSORAC Architecture

2.3.3 Architecture of RTSORAC

The RTSORAC model is built on a layered architecture that encapsulates various components responsible for real-time object-oriented database management aspects (Figure 2.9). In this section, we discuss the architecture of RTSORAC.

The layered architecture of RTSORAC comprises the following layers:

1. User Interface Layer
2. Real-Time Scheduling Layer
3. Active Rules Layer
4. Object-Oriented Database Layer

Each layer interacts with the adjacent layers to support real-time object-oriented database management. We will now discuss each layer in detail.

1. **User Interface Layer**: The User Interface Layer serves as the entry point for the users and applications to interact with the RTSORAC database. This layer is responsible for accepting user queries, transforming them into real-time transactions, and returning the results to the users or applications. The User Interface Layer also plays a crucial role in enforcing access control and security measures to protect the data stored in the database.
2. **Real-Time Scheduling Layer**: The Real-Time Scheduling Layer is responsible for managing the execution of real-time transactions while considering their timing constraints, such as deadlines and priorities. This layer integrates real-time scheduling algorithms, such as Earliest Deadline First (EDF) and Rate Monotonic Scheduling (RMS), to prioritize and schedule transactions according to their timing requirements. In addition, the Real-Time Scheduling Layer works closely with the Active Rules Layer and Object-Oriented Database Layer to ensure that transactions are executed within their deadlines while maintaining the consistency and integrity of the data.
3. **Active Rules Layer**: The Active Rules Layer manages the active rules associated with the database objects. These active rules, also known as triggers or Event-Condition-Action (ECA) rules, define the automatic actions that should be taken when specific events occur and certain conditions are met. The Active Rules Layer works in conjunction with the Real-Time Scheduling Layer to ensure that the active rules are executed within their deadlines and that their actions do not conflict with the ongoing transactions in the system.
4. **Object-Oriented Database Layer**: The Object-Oriented Database Layer is the core of the RTSORAC model and is responsible for storing, retrieving, and manipulating data as objects. This layer supports object-oriented features such as encapsulation, inheritance, and polymorphism, allowing for a more natural and expressive representation of real-world entities in the database. The Object-Oriented Database Layer is also responsible for implementing concurrency control mechanisms, such as locking and optimistic concurrency control, to ensure that transactions are executed in a manner that maintains the consistency and integrity of the data.

2.4 The COMET approach

COMET [110] is a customizable real-time embedded database platform designed to cater to the requirements of diverse real-time and embedded applications. In the rest of this section, we will discuss the pertinent aspects of the RTCOM model and aspect packages, as they play a crucial role in COMET's adaptability. Following that, we will explain how COMET can be adapted for different applications by incorporating new functionalities through aspect packages.

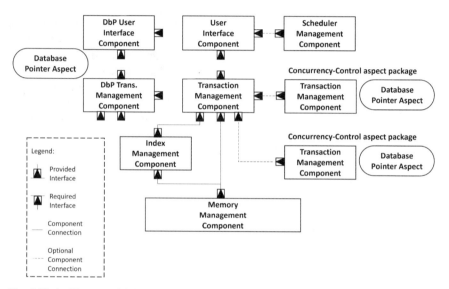

Fig. 2.10 Architecture of COMET with Aspect Packages

2.4.1 Components and Aspects

In COMET, tailorability mainly pertains to the adaptability of its software architecture (Figure 2.10), which is achieved by defining two fundamental and reusable architectural units: components and aspect packages. Components implement a portion of well-defined database functionality, demonstrating solid internal cohesion and weak coupling with other database functionality aspects. Furthermore, components are designed and implemented using a real-time component model (RTCOM) [109] and can be tailored through aspect weaving.

RTCOM outlines the design and implementation of components in a real-time environment, enabling the tailoring of components to meet the specific needs of an application while maintaining information hiding and facilitating component reuse and analysis of the system's temporal behavior, such as WCET analysis or formal verification using timed automata [112] [111]. RTCOM components in its architecture are "grey" as they are encapsulated in interfaces; however, aspects can predictably modify their behavior. Therefore, components offer an initial functionality that weaving aspects can alter or adjust. Each RTCOM component possesses two types of functional interfaces: provided and required. Provided interfaces represent a set of operations that a component offers to other components, while required interfaces denote a set of operations that the component needs (utilizes) from other components. The composition interface declares join points where component functionality changes can be made, thus defining locations where modifications can be applied within the component. Join points must be explicitly stated in a separate interface to ensure the system's evolution. Specifically, when developing new aspects, the aspect developer does not need complete knowledge of the component code to create aspects that can quickly and successfully tailor that component.

A composition of COMET components offering basic functionality is referred to as the basic COMET configuration (or simply basic COMET). For example, the primary database functionality refers to the minimal subset of database functionality that can constitute a working database. This minimal subset typically includes an interface for applications to access the database and functionality for defining and executing transactions that read and update data on physical storage. Consequently, the following COMET components are comprising basic COMET:

- component for user interface (UIC),
- component for scheduling management (SMC),
- component for indexing management (IMC),
- component for transaction management (TMC), and
- component for memory management (MMC).

The UIC offers an interface to the database for applications, allowing users (i.e., applications utilizing the database) to search and modify data elements. User requests are parsed by the user interface and transformed into an execution plan. The TMC is in charge of executing incoming execution plans, which ultimately manipulates the data. In addition, the IMC manages an index of all tuples within the database. Lastly, the SMC records transactions present in the system. It should be noted that the basic COMET configuration includes a fundamental data model and a basic transaction model. The primary data model comprises metadata utilized for concurrency control algorithms in databases. The basic transaction model describes each transaction τ_i solely by a period p_i and a relative deadline d_i. The basic COMET is particularly appropriate for small embedded vehicular systems [109].

2.4.2 Aspect Packages

Aspect packages implement new, non-basic functionalities that can be added to the existing database functionality, thus creating a new variant of the database system. All non-basic functionalities are considered to be features of the database. Elements in the real-time database domain typically include real-time policies that facilitate concurrent database access, various indexing strategies, enabling active behavior, and providing QoS guarantees, among others. Adding aspect packages to the basic COMET creates database configurations with new features. Consequently, an aspect package represents a method for packaging the specification and implementation of real-time features, such as concurrency control, QoS, indexing, and scheduling, for reuse and configuration.

At an abstract level, an aspect package specifies a real-time database feature, where a database feature is chosen independently of an application through aspects and components. At a concrete level, an aspect package comprises a set of aspects and (possibly empty) a set of components implementing an array of real-time policies. Components within the aspect package contain the core functional infrastructure of the features (policies), such as QoS management algorithms.

Moreover, three types of aspects are defined within an aspect package as follows.

• Transaction model aspects adjust the transaction model of a real-time database system to match the model employed by the policies by incorporating various attributes to transactions. For instance, a utilization transaction model is needed for a feedback-based QoS policy that controls system utilization.
• Policy aspects tailor the system to offer a range of related real-time policies, such as feedback-based QoS policies or concurrency control policies.
• Connector aspects enable the integration of an existing system with components from the aspect package.

System designers can use an aspect package to create multiple applications with similar features concerning a specific real-time policy. As a result, each group of applications would have its distinct aspect package.

In COMET the following aspect packages have been developed:

• The index aspect package implements indexing policies that promote efficient data access. The index aspect package consists of one component, an alternative IMC that implements the B-tree structure (IMC B-tree), and the aspect implementing the GUARD indexing policy.
• The concurrency control aspect package offers an implementation of various concurrency control policies, enabling the creation of a family of databases with distinct strategies for handling data conflicts. The concurrency control aspect package includes one component, the locking manager component (LCM), and aspects implementing high-priority two-phase locking (HP-2PL) and optimistic divergence control (ODC) protocols.
• The active behavior package allows the development of database system configurations that can respond to aperiodic events. It comprises aspects of implementing on-demand algorithms and ECA rules.
• The QoS aspect package includes a set of components and aspects that implement various feedback-based QoS policies. The QoS aspect package contains two components, the quality of service QoS admission controller component (QAC) and the feedback controller component (FCC), and the aspects implementing multiple feedback control-based quality of service policies.

Take note that while the content of an aspect package varies based on the functionality offered within the package, each package generally contains one or multiple aspects that implement a particular group of (related) policies. Furthermore, if a policy necessitates changes to COMET's transaction model, the package includes practical aspects that enhance this model. To demonstrate how the transaction and data model needs to be adapted for the employed policy, consider the FC-M and QMF QoS algorithms. These algorithms demand more sophisticated data and transaction models capable of capturing additional metadata such as average inter-arrival and execution times. Both FC-M and QMF require a transaction model where a transaction τ_i is categorized as either an update or a user transaction. Update transactions arrive periodically and can only write to the base (temporal) data objects. User transactions arrive aperiodically and may read temporal and read/write non-temporal data.

In this model, referred to as the utilization transaction model, each transaction possesses the following attributes:

- estimated execution time $x_{E,i}$,
- actual execution time $x_{A,i}$,
- period p_i (update transactions),
- estimated mean inter-arrival time $r_{E,i}$ (user transactions),
- actual mean inter-arrival time $r_{A,i}$ (user transactions),
- relative deadline d_i,
- estimated utilization $u_{E,i}$, and
- actual utilization $u_{A,i}$.

Attribute	Periodic Transactions	Aperiodic Transactions
d_i	$d_i = p_i$	$d_i = r_{A,i}$
$u_{E,i}$	$u_{E,i} = x_{E,i}/p_i$	$u_{E,i} = x_{E,i}/r_{E,i}$
$u_{A,i}$	$u_{A,i} = x_{A,i}/p_i$	$u_{A,i} = x_{A,i}/r_{A,i}$

Table 2.1 The utilization transaction model

Table 2.1 displays the entire utilization transaction model. When a transaction arrives, it presents the estimated average utilization $u_{E,i}$ and the relative deadline d_i to the system. However, the actual utilization of the transaction $u_{A,i}$ remains unknown in advance due to variations in execution time.

It is important to note that adding aspect packages to the basic COMET configuration is incremental. For example, when creating a QoS COMET configuration, the concurrency control aspect package should first be applied to the basic configuration. Subsequently, the appropriate index package (optional) can be added, and finally, aspects and components from the QoS aspect package can be utilized to configure the COMET QoS configuration.

2.5 Feedback Control-Based QoS Management on Real-Time Databases

Feedback Control-Based Quality of Service (QoS) Management is an approach to managing the performance and resource utilization of real-time database management systems (RTDBMS) by dynamically adjusting system parameters based on observed performance metrics [66]. This approach aims to achieve the desired QoS level by continuously monitoring system performance and adjusting the control parameters to maintain the system within its specified operating range.

Figure 2.11 shows the architecture.

2.5.1 Feedback Control Loop

The feedback control loop consists of four main components: a performance monitor, a performance analyzer, a decision maker, and an actuator.

- **Performance Monitor**: The performance monitor collects performance metrics from the RTDBMS, such as response time, throughput, and resource utilization. These metrics are used to evaluate the system's current performance against the desired QoS levels.
- **Performance Analyzer**: The performance analyzer processes the collected metrics and compares them with the desired QoS levels. If there is a deviation from the target QoS, the analyzer determines the cause and magnitude of the deviation.
- **Decision Maker**: The decision maker determines the necessary adjustments to the control parameters to achieve the desired QoS levels. This may involve increasing or decreasing resource allocation, adjusting task priorities, or other system adjustments.
- **Actuator**: The actuator applies the adjustments the decision maker determines to the system. This can involve modifying database schema, tuning system parameters, or changing the scheduling policy.

2.5.2 Controller Function

The following equation can represent a typical feedback control loop:

$$e(t) = r(t) - y(t) \tag{2.7}$$

where $e(t)$ is the error signal, $r(t)$ is the reference input (desired QoS level), and $y(t)$ is the output (actual performance metric). The control parameter adjustments are determined by a controller function, which can be represented as:

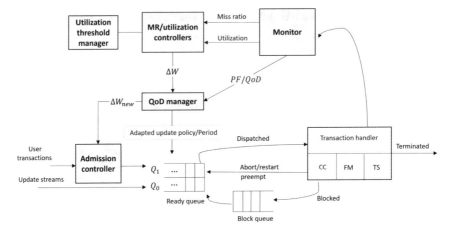

Fig. 2.11 RTDBS architecture for QoS management using feedback control

$$u(t) = K_p e(t) + K_i \int e(t)dt + K_d \frac{de(t)}{dt} \qquad (2.8)$$

where $u(t)$ is the control parameter adjustment, K_p, K_i, and K_d are the proportional, integral, and derivative gains, respectively. These gains can be tuned to achieve the desired performance characteristics, such as minimizing overshoot, reducing steady-state error, and improving transient response.

2.5.3 Applications in Real-Time Database Management Systems

Feedback Control-Based QoS Management has been applied in various RTDBMS applications, including:

- **Adaptive deadline assignment for real-time transactions** [80]: In this application, feedback control is used to dynamically adjust transaction deadlines based on the current system workload and resource availability. This helps to maintain the desired transaction response time and throughput.
- **Load shedding in data stream management systems** [108]: In this context, feedback control is employed to dynamically adjust the amount of data processed by the system in response to fluctuations in input data rates and system resource availability. This helps to maintain the desired processing latency and output data quality.
- **Dynamic resource allocation for distributed real-time systems** [115]: Here , feedback control is utilized to dynamically allocate resources, such as CPU, memory, and network bandwidth, among distributed real-time tasks based on their current demands and priorities. This ensures that the desired performance

metrics, such as deadline satisfaction and resource utilization, are maintained across the distributed system.

2.5.4 Advantages and Challenges

Feedback Control-Based QoS Management offers several advantages in the context of RTDBMS:

- **Adaptability**: The feedback control loop allows the system to adapt to changing workloads and resource availability in real-time, ensuring that the desired QoS levels are maintained even under varying conditions.
- **Robustness**: By continuously monitoring and adjusting system parameters, the feedback control loop can help to mitigate the impact of unexpected disturbances, such as hardware failures or sudden workload spikes.
- **Tunability**: The controller function can be tuned to achieve the desired performance characteristics, enabling system designers to balance trade-offs between performance metrics, such as response time, throughput, and resource utilization.

However, there are also several challenges associated with implementing Feedback Control-Based QoS Management in RTDBMS:

- **Modeling Complexity**: Developing accurate models of the system's performance and resource utilization can be challenging, particularly for complex systems with multiple interacting components and varying workloads.
- **Control Stability**: Ensuring the stability of the feedback control loop is critical for maintaining the desired QoS levels. Poorly tuned controller parameters can result in oscillatory behavior, slow convergence, or instability.
- **Implementation Overhead**: Implementing the feedback control loop requires additional computational resources for monitoring, analyzing, and adjusting system parameters. This overhead must be carefully managed to avoid negatively impacting the system's performance.

Despite these challenges, Feedback Control-Based QoS Management has proven to be a practical approach for maintaining desired performance levels in various real-time database management systems. By continuously monitoring and adjusting system parameters, this approach ensures that the RTDBMS can adapt to changing workloads and maintain the desired QoS levels under a wide range of operating conditions.

2.5.5 Feedback Control Techniques

Several feedback control techniques have been proposed in the literature to address the challenges associated with implementing Feedback Control-Based QoS Management in RTDBMS. Some of the prominent techniques include:

- **Proportional-Integral-Derivative (PID) Control** [66]: The PID controller is a widely used feedback control technique that combines the proportional, integral, and derivative terms of the error signal to compute the control parameter adjustments. PID controllers are known for their simplicity, robustness, and adaptability, making them a popular choice for various applications, including RTDBMS.
- **Model Predictive Control (MPC)** [84]: MPC is an advanced feedback control technique that relies on a model of the system to predict its future behavior and compute optimal control parameter adjustments. By taking into account the future impact of the control decisions, MPC can provide better performance compared to conventional feedback control techniques at the expense of increased computational complexity.
- **Adaptive Control** [43]: Adaptive control techniques adjust the controller parameters in real-time based on the observed system behavior. This enables the controller to adapt to changes in the system dynamics or operating conditions, ensuring optimal performance under varying workloads and resource availability.
- **Fuzzy Control** [107]: Fuzzy control techniques use fuzzy logic to model the complex relationships between system variables and control parameters. By representing the control rules using linguistic terms and fuzzy sets, fuzzy controllers can handle the inherent uncertainties and nonlinearities in the system, providing a more flexible and robust control solution.

2.6 QeDB: A Quality-Aware Embedded Real-Time Database

QeDB [47] serves as a database tailored for data-driven real-time applications operating on embedded systems with flash memory. Embedded system databases function on a best-effort basis, offering no assurance regarding timeliness or data freshness. Additionally, traditional real-time database (RTDB) technologies cannot be adapted to these embedded databases, as they assume that a system's primary memory can accommodate the entire database, which is not feasible for data-intensive real-time applications. Instead, QeDB employs an innovative feedback control strategy to ensure QoS in embedded systems without necessitating that all data be stored in the main memory. Specifically, their methodology focuses on the concurrent management of both I/O and CPU resources to achieve the required timeliness.

2.6.1 System Model

QeDB is designed for real-time embedded systems that utilize high-capacity flash memory as secondary storage. The software stack of an embedded system running a real-time application with RTEDB support is depicted in Figure 2.12. A buffer in the main memory serves as a cache between the CPU and the slower secondary storage. This buffer is shared globally among transactions to decrease data access time. If an application's I/O request for a data object is not found in the buffer, I/O operations to the flash memory are triggered.

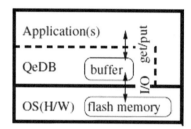

Fig. 2.12 Software Stack of a Real-Time Application with RTEDB support

2.6.2 Data and Transactions

Contrary to conventional DBMSs, QeDB does not facilitate intricate data query processing. Instead, it functions as a key/value store, enabling efficient and simultaneous access to data. Moreover, QeDB employs the underlying Berkeley DB's data storage and retrieval mechanism with minimal modification.

The interface put(key k_1, value v) is utilized for storing data v with key k_1, while the interface gets (key k_2) retrieves data associated with key k_2. Operations get and put primarily involve I/O operations between the buffer and secondary storage for fetching and flushing data. However, they also necessitate computation for tasks such as buffer cache manipulation, index lookup, and data and index page locking. In QeDB, I/O operations pertain to put-and-get operations, encompassing raw I/O operations to flash memory and the computation required for these I/O operations.

Data objects within QeDB can be categorized into two groups: temporal and non-temporal data. Temporal data objects undergo periodic updates by update transactions. For instance, an update transaction is initiated when a new sensor reading is available. Conversely, user transactions may access and modify both temporal and non-temporal data objects unlike update transactions. All transactions are predefined canned transactions, with operations determined during the application's design phase. These operations are hard-coded into the applications and dynamically invoked at runtime. While a transaction's characteristics, such as execution time and access pattern, are known during the design phase, the overall database workload and data access pattern are unpredictable and change dynamically. This is because the invocation frequency of each transaction is unknown, and multiple transactions execute concurrently. As a result, their response time can be uncertain. Transactions access data through QeDB; if applications specify them, transactional properties like ACID (atomicity, consistency, isolation, and durability) are provided between data accesses.

2.6.3 Real-Time Transactions

Transactions can be divided into real-time and non-real-time transactions. Real-time transactions have deadlines for completion and hold a higher priority than non-real-time transactions. For example, in Program 1, the transaction must report the structural integrity status of a burning building within a specified deadline; failure to do so could result in firefighters losing the opportunity to evacuate a potentially collapsing location. Soft deadline semantics is adopted, where transactions retain value even if they miss their deadline. For instance, receiving a delayed report on the building's condition is preferable to not receiving any information due to transaction abortion.

Soft deadline semantics are selected because most data-intensive real-time applications accessing databases are inherently soft real-time applications. However, due to concurrent data access and complex interactions, such as database locking, achieving hard real-time can be challenging. Therefore, this paper primarily focuses on QoS management that dynamically reduces the tardiness of these real-time transactions during runtime.

2.6.4 Performance Metrics

The system's objective is to maintain QoS at a specific level. In real-time systems, the deadline-miss ratio is a prevalent QoS metric. Transaction deadlines are application-specific requirements concerning transaction timeliness. The deadline miss ratio represents the proportion of late transactions to total transactions. However, the deadline-miss ratio has proven problematic in RTEDBs because the transaction invocation rate in embedded databases is much lower than in traditional database systems, which handle thousands of transactions per second. For instance, a firefighter's PDA real-time transaction checking the building's status might be invoked per second. The deadline miss ratio's confidence interval can be substantial with such a limited number of transactions. Instead, QeDB controls QoS based on the transactions' average tardiness. For each transaction, tardiness is defined as the ratio of the transaction's response time to its corresponding (relative) deadline.

$$tardiness = \frac{response - time}{deadline} \qquad (2.9)$$

Another QoS metric, which may present conflicting requirements, is data freshness. In RTDBs, validity intervals are utilized to maintain temporal consistency between the database's real-world state and sensor data. A sensor data object O_i is considered fresh or temporally consistent if the current $time - timestamp(O_i) \leq avi(O_i)$, where $avi(O_i)$ is the absolute validity interval of O_i. To support sensor data freshness, the update period is set to $P_i = 0.5 \times avi(O_i)$ for O_i. QeDB keeps the desired data freshness regarding perceived freshness (PF).

$$PF = \frac{N_{fresh}}{N_{accessed}} \qquad (2.10)$$

where N_{fresh} denotes the number of fresh data accessed by real-time transactions, and N_{access} signifies the total number of data accessed by real-time transactions. Data freshness could be traded off when overloaded to enhance tardiness, provided the target freshness is not breached.

2.6.5 I/O deadline and CPU deadline

A transaction's tardiness is influenced by the response time of both I/O operations and computation within the transaction. Specifically, I/O response time is crucial in data-intensive real-time applications. Although the transaction's tardiness in the Equation reveals the extent of system overload, it does not indicate which resource is overloaded, either I/O or CPU. Consequently, a transaction's deadline is divided into I/O and CPU deadlines to assess the tardiness of I/O and CPU activities separately. In a transaction, the I/O deadline and CPU deadline represent the maximum total time allocated to all I/O operations and all computational activities, respectively. Initially, the transaction's I/O deadline and CPU deadline are determined based on the profiled minimum execution time of I/O operations, $EXEC\_i/o$, and the computational activities, $EXEC\_cpu$. $EXEC_{i/o}$ comprises overhead proportional to the number of I/O operations, such as buffer cache lookup and index/data page locking. Still, it does not include the actual I/O time for accessing data in flash memory since the buffer hit ratio is assumed to be 100%. $EXEC_{cpu}$ is the minimum execution time of the transaction, excluding $EXEC_{i/o}$. Given $EXEC_{i/o}$ and $EXEC_{cpu}$, the transaction's slack time can be calculated:

$$(EXEC_{i/o} + EXEC_{cpu}) \times sf = deadline \qquad (2.11)$$

Here, sf represents the slack factor, which should be greater than one for a transaction to be schedulable in the given system. Thus, the initial I/O deadline and CPU deadline are set as follows:

$$deadline_{i/o} = EXEC_{i/o} \times sf \qquad (2.12)$$

$$deadline_{\text{cpu}} = EXEC_{\text{cpu}} \times sf = deadline - deadline_{\text{i/o}} \qquad (2.13)$$

The tardiness Equation is expanded to include I/O and CPU tardiness as follows:

$$tardiness_{i/o} = response_time_{i/o}deadline_{i/o} \qquad (2.14)$$

$$tardiness_{cpu} = response_time_{cpu}deadline - cpu \qquad (2.15)$$

Nonetheless, assigning the same static slack factor to both I/O and CPU deadlines can be problematic, as the optimal slack times for I/O operations and computation vary with system status changes. For example, if one resource is overloaded while the other is not, it would be preferable to allocate more slack time to the overloaded resource, as the other resource is under-utilized. To address this issue, QeDB dynamically adjusts I/O and CPU deadlines in each sampling period using Algorithm 7.

Algorithm 7 Run-time adaptation of deadlines

Require: average tardiness$_{i/o}$ and tardiness$_{cpu}$
Require: $\Delta_{i/o}$ and Δ_{cpu}
 1: **if** tardiness$_{i/o} \leq$ tardiness$_{cpu}$ **then**
 2:      $\Delta_{i/o}$ += 1
 3:      Δ_{cpu} = 0
 4:      $\delta d = k \times \Delta_{i/o}$
 5:      increase deadline$_{i/o}$ by $\delta d\%$
 6: **else**
 7:      Δ_{cpu} += 1
 8:      $\Delta_{i/o}$ = 0
 9:      $\delta d = k \times \Delta_{cpu}$
10:      decrease deadline$_{i/o}$ by $\delta d\%$
11: **end if**
12: deadline$_{cpu}$ = deadline $-$ deadline$_{i/o}$

In Algorithm 7, I/O and CPU deadlines are modified by $\delta d\%$ during each sampling period. Under normal circumstances, δd is set to 1 in the experimental setup. However, when a particular resource experiences consecutive overload periods, δd increases multiplicatively to expedite the deadline adaptation process. When the QoS controller is active, consecutive overloading of a specific resource occurs when the QoS controller is unable to adjust the CPU or I/O load further.

2.6.6 QoS Management Architecture

Figure 2.13 illustrates the QeDB architecture, which is composed of a MIMO feedback controller, actuator, performance monitor, admission controller, buffer manager

(BM), concurrency controller (CC), and scheduler (SC). The figure presents three distinct queues within the ready queue. Temporal data updates are assigned to Q0 and given the highest priority. Real-time user transactions are managed in Q1, while non-real-time transactions in Q_2 hold the lowest priority and are only dispatched if Q_0 and Q_1 are empty. Transactions in each queue are scheduled based on a first-come-first-served (FCFS) approach. When a user transaction arrives, it must be completed within a timeframe equal to the current time plus its (relative) deadline. For concurrency control, QeDB utilizes the two-phase locking (2PL) method provided by the underlying Berkeley DB. As a result, transactions may experience blocking, abortion, or restarting due to data conflicts.

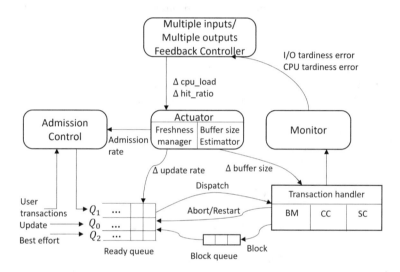

Fig. 2.13 QeDB Architecture

In determining transaction priorities, both transaction timeliness and data freshness present conflicting demands. If user transactions are assigned a higher priority than temporal updates, transaction timeliness may be enhanced at the expense of a potential reduction in data freshness and vice versa. In QeDB, temporal data updates are given higher priority to maintain data freshness. Nonetheless, the timeliness of user transactions is still ensured by the feedback control loop, which regulates the update transaction rate and buffer size. First, the performance monitor calculates the I/O and CPU tardiness, or the discrepancy between the desired I/O (and CPU) response time and the observed I/O (and CPU) response time, at each sampling period. Using these errors, the feedback controller computes the necessary buffer hit ratio adjustment (Δhit ratio) and CPU load adjustment (Δcpu load). Next, the actuator estimates the required buffer size adjustment and update rate adjustment based on Δhit ratio and Δcpu load. Lastly, the buffer and freshness managers modify the buffer size and update rates for temporal data.

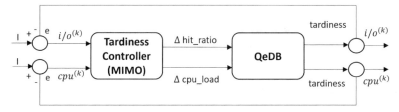

Fig. 2.14 Tardiness Control Loop

The objective of the feedback controller depicted in Figure 2.14 is to maintain the transaction response time equal to its deadline, necessitating a desired tardiness of 1. The overall feedback control process is as follows:

1. At the kth sampling instant, the tardiness errors $e_{i/o}(k)$ and $e_{cpu}(k)$ are calculated for I/O tardiness and CPU tardiness, respectively.
2. Using $e_{i/o}(k)$ and $e_{cpu}(k)$, the MIMO controller computes the control signals Δhit ratio and Δcpu load. In contrast to a Single Input/Single Output (SISO) controller, the MIMO controller concurrently calculates control signals, considering both I/O tardiness and CPU tardiness.
3. The actuator converts Δhit ratio to Δbuffer size. QeDB employs a linear model that associates buffer size with buffer hit ratio. This linear model is updated at each sampling period since data access locality dynamically changes during runtime. The buffer size is modified according to this model to achieve Δbuffer size. Altering the buffer size also impacts CPU load, as demonstrated in the following section. Consequently, Δcpu load is adjusted after implementing a new buffer size.
4. The Δcpu load is obtained by modifying the update rates of cold temporal data. Update transactions have minimal influence on the buffer hit ratio since they only access one data object. For efficient temporal data updates, the access update ratio AUR$[i]$ is computed for each temporal data d_i; AUR$[i]$ is defined as Access Frequency$[i]$. If Δcpu load < 0, the update rates of a cold data object, accessed infrequently, are adjusted from $p[i]$ to $p[i]$new. The adjustment alters CPU load by $(p[i]\text{new} - p[i])/p[i]$. This update period adjustment continues for a subset of cold data until Δcpu load ≥ 0 or no further freshness adaptation is feasible.

2.7 RT-MongoDB: A NoSQL Database Solution

Over the past decade, the importance and transformative capabilities of cloud computing have become increasingly evident, especially in the realm of contemporary web application development. This technology offers considerable benefits to businesses of all sizes by eliminating the necessity for investment in dedicated data centers. While numerous studies [11,58] apply high-performance computing methods to distributed and cloud applications for optimal performance, few works focus on delivering customizable end-to-end service-level objectives with varying quality of service (QoS) for different users or clients. The trade-off between throughput and response time becomes clear when designing services that must balance maximizing throughput and quickly addressing asynchronous real-time requests. The former requires approaches that consolidate many requests into large batches for processing with minimal overheads and utilize long intermediate buffers to reduce worker thread idle times. On the other hand, the latter demands preemptible, short-lived tasks that can be paused in favor of higher-priority ones and the usage of small buffers to minimize individual request processing latency. Developing distributed software systems that find the right equilibrium between these requirements is more challenging. Circumstances that would benefit the most from a design that supports differentiated performance per user or request involve those where a broad range of applications must submit requests to the same component(s). One example is a cloud data center database system that must handle heavyweight requests for batch or high-performance applications while attending to lightweight requests from soft real-time applications that demand quick responses to user interactions or asynchronous conditions, such as online gaming or collaborative document editing. This work tackles the issue in the context of storage systems by using the prioritized access principle, a commonly employed trade-off in real-time system design. Higher-priority tasks are given resources before lower-priority ones, sometimes even preempting them by withdrawing their resource access mid-task or starving them for extended durations. Although priority-based access alone is insufficient to guarantee predictable performance, integrating it with solid real-time design principles and analysis can ensure the proper functioning and sufficient resources for all hosted real-time tasks [20]. In this context, NoSQL database services are emerging as a vital technology for replicated and infinitely scalable data storage solutions, primarily due to their typically lower consistency and functionality requirements compared to relational alternatives.

2.7.1 Fundamental Concepts

MongoDB is an open-source, document-oriented data storage system widely praised in comparative research [73] for its versatility and user-friendliness while offering all the essential features to address the complex requirements of modern applications. The term *mongodb* stems from humongous, meaning extremely large, highlighting its ability to store and manage substantial amounts of data. Effectively handling large-scale traffic, a common necessity for content delivery services, is a challenge for relational database technologies to achieve effortlessly. For instance, MongoDB's access speed is ten times faster than MySQL's when data exceeds 50GB [85]. Moreover, *mongodb* employs BSON, a binary-encoded serialization of JSON, for document storage, which is designed to optimize storage space and scanning speed.

A BSON document comprises multiple named fields, including an automatically generated identifier for unique identification. Each field contains a name, a data type, and a value. BSON supports complex JSON data types, such as arrays and nested documents, as well as other types, like binary, integer, floating point, and date time. Documents are stored in schemaless tables, referred to as collections, which allow heterogeneous documents to coexist within the same collection (although the similarity is recommended for index efficiency). Users interact with the database system using a JSON-based query language offered by API libraries or drivers, compatible with all major programming languages. *mongodb* ensures data durability and availability and enables horizontal scaling through replication and sharding. Replication involves deploying multiple physical copies of the same database to form a replica set. On the other hand, sharding consists in deploying a cluster of distinct databases, called a sharded cluster, each containing subsets of data distributed based on user-defined criteria.

2.7.1.1 MongoDB Internals

This section provides an overview of the internal components and mechanisms of *mongodb* software that have been explored and the integration of the proposed approach with them. Here version 4.2 is considered, which can be found on GitHub7.

MongoDB is structured as a customizable client-server architecture. The primary component is the *mongodb* service, responsible for core database operations such as processing requests, updating the storage unit, and managing logging processes. The approach is built upon two design choices related to the default execution model and concurrency control mechanism employed by a *mongod* instance. These choices enable the smooth integration of modifications into the core software with minimal overhead:

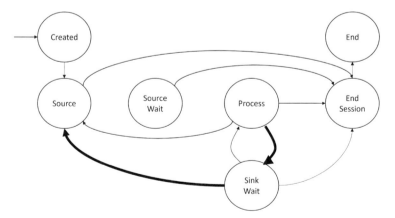

Fig. 2.15 Life-cycle FSM of a client connection session.

1. **Mongodb manages network connections synchronously**: each incoming connection is allocated a dedicated server-side client worker thread in charge of handling database operations and overseeing the session life-cycle. Worker threads
   adhere to a finite-state machine (FSM) workflow. The primary request-response
   interaction involves multiple passes through the transition path known as Standard RPC, aligning with these events: await the client request, process the request,
   wait for the result from the storage unit, and transmit a response (Figure 2.15).
   The thread is relinquished when the connection terminates. In *mongodb* Version
   4.2, it is safe to assume that every incoming connection has its own dedicated
   server-side worker thread.
2. **Mongodb employs an optimistic version of the Multiversion Concurrency
   Control mechanism** ([13]), allowing for concurrent write operations without
   locks. Data consistency is maintained by presenting users with a snapshot of the
   database at a specific moment. Changes a writer makes are exposed to other users
   once the operation concludes without conflicts. Write conflicts that occur due to
   concurrent updates to the same document are resolved by confirming one write
   operation and transparently retrying any others. Multiple *mongod* services can
   function on distinct physical machines and be connected via a simple socket-
   based, request-response styled protocol named MongoDBWire Protocol for more
   complex deployments providing data redundancy and/or horizontal scalability. A
   collection of independent *mongod* instances, which maintain an identical data set,
   is called a replica set. The primary node oversees all write operations and records
   data set alterations in an operation log (oplog); secondary nodes mirror the primary's oplog and asynchronously apply changes to their local copies. Replica
   set members communicate frequently using heartbeat messages to identify and
   adapt to topology changes. For example, if the primary node becomes inaccessi-
   ble, the replica set commences an election process to select a new primary. The
   primary election and oplog replication processes are founded on a variant of the
   RAFT consensus algorithm ([72]). The oplog, a fixed-size collection stored in
   the *mongod* instance, treats records as regular documents but with a fixed structure. Oplog entries detail data set alterations in an idempotent manner. They are
   uniquely identified by the opTime field, a tuple containing a timestamp, and a
   node-specific term that identifies the primary node responsible for the write operation. This field dictates the order of operations. A secondary mongod instance
   replicates the oplog using the subsequent components (illustrated in Figure 2.16):
   The replication process pipeline. functions as follows: a secondary node retrieves
   oplog entries from the primary node and accumulates them in batches within a
   buffer. Subsequently, these entries are extracted and organized into another set of
   batches that the writer threads can concurrently apply. These writer threads then
   modify both the local copy of the secondary's oplog and the database.

• The OplogFetcher acquires oplog entries from the primary by executing find
  and getMore commands at the same endpoint as a user connection. Entries are
  obtained in batches and saved in a buffer known as the OplogBuffer.

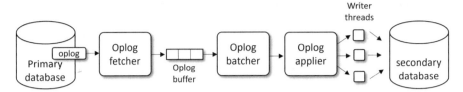

Fig. 2.16 The replication process pipeline.

- The OplogBatcher extracts fetched batches from the OplogBuffer and constructs the subsequent batch of operations to be implemented on the local data set replica.
- The OplogApplier is responsible for applying the batches generated by the Oplog-Batcher to the local oplog and storage unit. It manages a pool of writer threads that, for improved performance, can use operations within a batch concurrently, possibly overlooking their chronological sequence. Consequently, specific operations require individual batches, such as the "drop" operation. Once a secondary node finishes replicating a batch, it notifies the primary node of the opTime of the last applied entry. This is crucial in cases where users request a particular degree of data durability, called the write-concern level in *mongodb* parlance. The primary node will await a specified number of notifications before acknowledging a write operation, confirming that the alteration has been replicated across a sufficient number of nodes. A high write concern value diminishes throughput, while a low value heightens the possibility of data loss during a failure. The write concern is commonly configured to ensure that most replicas have securely saved the data before responding to the client. A comparable feature, the read concern, is accessible for read operations and is employed to control data consistency. Both settings should be adapted to suit the application's needs.

2.7.2 RT-MONGODB

The RT-MongoDB [10] software is a modified version of *mongodb* that incorporates a prioritization scheme for simultaneous requests. This is accomplished by enabling users to manipulate the niceness value of the underlying client worker thread handling their requests, thereby modifying the thread scheduling sequence based on user requirements. To simplify, the range of niceness values is limited to three levels: high-priority (-20), normal-priority (0), and low-priority (+19).

The synchronous execution model facilitates straightforward identification of the target thread without side effects, enabling high-priority users and high-priority worker threads to be used interchangeably. However, prioritization by merely decreasing the niceness value for high-priority sessions may prove more effective in replicated situations where data durability is mandated. To tackle this issue, RT-MongoDB employs a soft checkpoint system that temporarily denies CPU access to lower-priority worker threads, consisting of two primitives: check-in and check-out, which are implemented in the client session's life cycle to mark the start and end points of the Standard RPC transition path. The objective is to create a prioritized access channel for completing high-priority requests by putting lower-priority worker threads to sleep during the necessary time window. To accomplish this, each worker thread announces its niceness level before processing a user request and may be halted by the checkpoint system if higher-priority requests are executed. Upon completing a request, a worker thread utilizes the check-out primitive to inform blocked threads and awaken them if no higher-priority requests are ongoing (Figure 2.17). The term "soft" indicates that this mechanism does not disrupt threads serving users who want to specify a different priority level, service threads created by the database for deployment management, or worker threads serving secondary nodes. The checkpoint system offers a prioritized channel to high-priority sessions by temporarily limiting CPU access to lower-priority ones. The identical finite-state machine is integrated with the checkpoint system (Figure 2.17). The check-in primitive specifies the niceness value of the underlying worker threads about to serve their clients. If higher-priority threads are executing, the checkpoint system will block them. The check-out primitive informs the checkpoint system of the completion of a Standard RPC path, which in turn will awaken lower-priority threads if no higher-priority ones are running.

In terms of API, RT-MongoDB has incorporated a new database command, *setClientPriority*, and an updated version of the *runCommand* command to facilitate differentiated performance on a per-user and per-request basis, respectively. Both commands employ the same mechanisms, execute the same tasks, and support all operations. However, the priority specified by *runCommand* persists only for a single Standard RPC transition, enabling temporary prioritization of the client session. On the other hand, *setClientPriority* designates the priority for all subsequent requests until the session is terminated or the priority is modified once more.

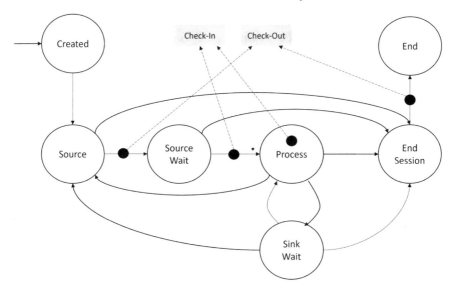

Fig. 2.17 Finite-state machine integrated with the checkpoint system.

2.8 V4DB Real-Time Database Testbed

According to V4DB designers [53], up to 2007, the major part of RTDB research was focused on the evolution and evaluation of transaction processing algorithms, priority assignment strategies, and concurrency control techniques. The evaluation was usually based on simulation studies except for a few exceptions. Simulations often consist of a number of parameters. The parameters specify the maximal count of data items, the average count of one transaction data page, processor time needed to manipulate data items, average disk access time, probability of read vs. write transaction, etc. There is even a study where all the functional blocks are designed as object-oriented and described by means of classes with a number of attributes. Much less attention was paid to architecture aspects of the operating systems, developed especially for real-time systems and for better support of time-critical operations. So two basic drawbacks of the presented research, up to 2007, can be defined:

1. For the most part, only one functional part is considered for investigation without any interaction with other system parts. Because of the strong interactions among the various processing components in RTDBS, an integrated approach is necessary.
2. Research work in real-time transaction processing is based on simulation studies only. It is necessary to investigate the real-time transaction processing algorithms in their natural environment to achieve really relevant results. It means that the operating platform for RTDBS is a real-time operating system, and the particular functional blocks communicate with each other by means of this operating system.

2.8.1 The V4DB System

The system is currently implemented upon the real-time operating system platform VxWorks as a centralized system with a memory resident database. The overall design is presented on Figure 2.18. Oval blocks represent parallel processes while the square blocks are single functional blocks within processes. Some of the system parts contain grayed blocks. The blocks illustrate the possibility of functionality change of the parts. Their runtime behaviour can be changed.

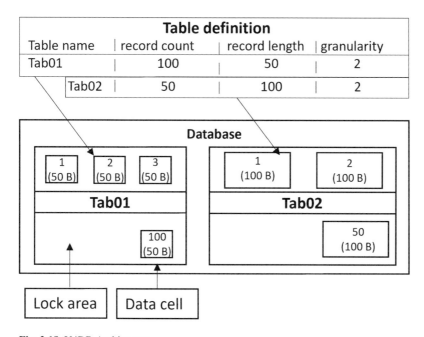

Fig. 2.18 V4DB Architecture

The main components of the architecture are the following:

1. **Predispatching**: After the admission, the transactions are predispatched. Predis-patching includes admission control to avoid system overloading and creating the transaction info-structure. The structure fully describes the transaction definition and all its parameters.
2. bf Dispatching: In the next step, the transaction parameters are extracted and dispatched for execution as to the priority assignment policy and the way of transaction processing. The priority assigned to a transaction execution process is mapped to a real operating system process priority, and the context (transaction) switching relies on an underlying operating system. This is one of the most important experimental system aspects.

3. **Processing**: When the transaction is scheduled for execution, first it is parsed into particular commands and then the commands are processed by the command executor. Database access must be synchronized through the concurrency control. The DBQuery block executes the commands on a logical level while the resource manager and memory manager work with physical data structures that are described by the data dictionary. To obtain reasonable performance, multiple transactions must be able to access data concurrently. So before a transaction performs an operation on a data object, it must be processed by concurrency control component in order to achieve the required synchronization.

2.8.2 V4DB Database

The project objective as an experimental system and application categories where RTDBS are used to advantage a simple schema is adopted in the following form: The database is divided into a predefined count of memory areas. Each area represents some table and consists of a predefined count of records. Records are of the same length for one memory area table just for simplicity. The database schema is outlined on Figure 2.19.

In V4DB, the database schema is defined by the notation:

```
tab name | rec count | rec byte length
```

for example: $Tab01|100|50$, means that there exists a table named Tab01 which has 100 records, each of 50 bytes in length.

2.8.3 Database granularity

The granularity parameter can be defined for each table mentioned above. The parameter stands for the count of logical areas into which each table is divided for the needs of concurrency control during transaction processing. The granularity is defined separately for each table, so the parameter can be added to the table definition and the final database schema looks like that:

```
tab name | rec count | rec byte length | granularity
```

for example, $Tab01|100|50|2$, means that there exists a table named Tab01 which has 100 records, each of 50 bytes in length; the table is divided into two logical areas according to granularity 2.

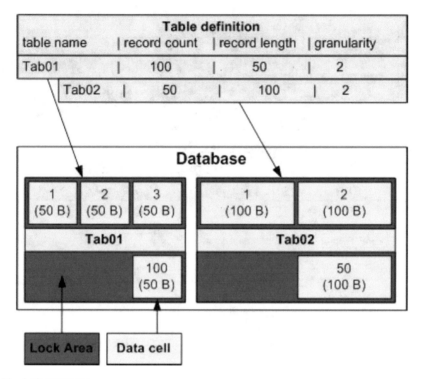

Fig. 2.19 V4DB Schema.

2.8.4 Description of the Transactions

Internal generators generate transactions. To study database transaction processing, it must be able to generate transactions whose properties are known and set in advance. The parameters are described in Figure 2.20.

Logical database access results from physical database design. Access to the second record of table 2.2 can be written as $Tab01 : 2$, etc. Next, four basic database access methods must be distinguished.

DB operation	Shortcut
Select	S
Update	U
Insert	I
Delete	D

Table 2.2 Shortcuts of DB operations

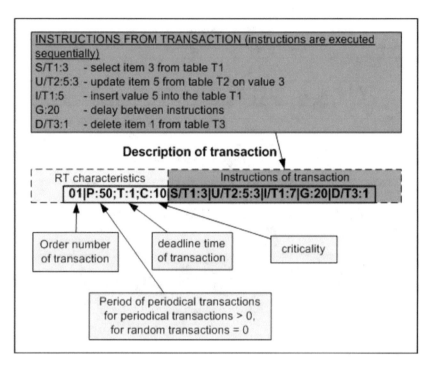

Fig. 2.20 V4DB Transactions.

For example, to select Tab01:2, it can be simply written as S/Tab01:2. Besides these basic principles, the real-time parameters in Table 2.3 further specify the transaction.

DB operation	Shortcut
Deadline	T
Period	P
Criticality	C

Table 2.3 Shortcuts of transaction's RT characteristics

2.8.5 System Test Options

The system is implemented upon the real-time operating system VxWorks. Currently, it includes all necessary core database and transaction services, admission control, priority assignment, and concurrency control. The way of operation of some system components can be changed according to project goals to enable testing the system behavior under different conditions. The test options currently include the following:

- **Variable database definition and granularity**: Database consists of tables defined by text lines in an external text file. Each table can be divided into predefined count of logical areas. Database schema is loaded during the system start.
- **Periodic and random transactions**: Transactions are defined by simple text files. Each line represents the definition of one transaction as described above. The file is loaded before the initialization of the generators.
- **Priority assignment strategy**: The priority assignment strategies make use of the RT characteristics of the transaction. There are four types implemented:

  1. **Deadline Monotonic (DM)**: Lower deadline = higher priority.
  2. **Most Criticality First (MCF)**: Higher criticality = higher priority.
  3. **Criticality Deadline First (CDF)**: Deadline-criticality 50-50 (%).
  4. **Random (RAND)**: uniformly generated random level of priority.

  The priority assigned to a transaction is mapped to a real operating system process priority.

2.8.5.1 Transaction Processing Type

How the transactions are executed has certainly a significant impact on system performance. V4DB supports two types of transaction execution:

1. **1 transaction = 1 process**: Each transaction is executed within its process. The process is created after transaction admission and destroyed after transaction commit. This processing type is used across all the experiments.
2. **2) Process pool**: The predefined count of processes executes the transactions. Each of the processes executes transactions within the specified range of priorities. This processing type is currently under development.

2.8.5.2 Concurrency Control Mode

In V4DB, there are two types of pessimistic 2PL (two-phase locking) and two types of optimistic protocols implemented, together with simple serial execution:

1. **Strict 2PL (2PL-STRICT)**: Locking protocol. Hold all locks until the end of the transaction without any change of transaction priority.
2. **2PL Wait-Promote (2PL-WP)**: The scheme is identical to the basic 2PL in resolving conflicts. But with this mechanism, whenever a request is blocked behind a lower-priority lock holder, the lock holder's priority is promoted to that of the requester.
3. **Optimistic locking - forward validation (OCC-FV)**: the transactions conflicted with the validating transaction are restarted.

4. **Optimistic sacrified validation (OCC-SAC)**: If the validating transaction conflicts with other transactions, it is restarted.
5. **Strict serial (SERIAL)**: Transactions are executed in order of their admission. No transaction preemption can occur.

2.9 Chronos Testbed

Chronos [48] is a testbed for RTDB systems that use the typical schema and workload of an Online Stock Trading system. Kang et al. developed this testbed in a joint effort by the State University of New York at Binghamton and the University of Virginia in 2007.

A Stock Trading System can be characterized as a soft real-time application [48]. In this type of system, many clients are trying to do some operations in their stock investments. A database is an ideal match for this type of system due to the required ACID support. Additionally, these transactions need to be processed within a specified delay bound.

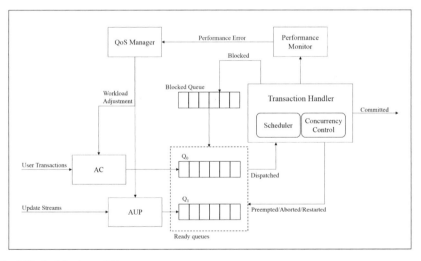

Fig. 2.21 Architecture of Chronos

2.9.1 Architecture of Chronos

In Chronos, individual transactions are not assigned separate deadlines. Instead, the idea is to process as many trade transactions as possible within a system-wide delay bound. The architecture of Chronos is presented in figure 2.21.

Chronos models two types of transactions:

1. **System Periodic Transactions.** These transactions are used to maintain the freshness of the data accessed by user transactions. They are enqueued in the queue Q_0, which receives a higher priority (compared to user transactions) to achieve the mentioned freshness.
2. **User Transactions.** As the name implies, these transactions are executed by the system users, potentially using the data refreshed by the periodic transactions. They are enqueued in Q_1, which receives a lower priority than those enqueued in Q_0.

Transactions in each queue Q_0 and Q_1 are scheduled in *First-Come First-Served* (FCFS) fashion under *Two-Phase Locking* (2PL). Transactions might be blocked, aborted, or restarted. A blocked transaction is appended to the *block queue* shown in figure 2.21. Two of the proposals in the paper are the **QoS Manager** plus the **Performance Monitor Module**. Together, they periodically compute the difference between the response time of transactions and the desired delay. Based on that, some actions are taken as *Admission Control* or *Adaptive Updates*. These two actions are described in detail in the paper.

2.9.2 Client-Server Application

Chronos is a client-server application. Clients submit a connection request to the server, and at some point, the server accepts the request and creates a connection, allocating a server-side thread. Subsequently, the client is allowed to send transaction requests. Then, the request is received by the server-side thread and processed. Once processed, the result is returned to the suspended client waiting for this reply. In the model presented in the paper, after the client-side thread receives the server's response, it remains a *think time* before submitting a new request, following the idea of the **TPC-C**, the online transaction processing benchmark.

The Chronos testbed has eight tables, but only four tables are accessed in the experiments reported in [48]: *Stocks, Quotes, Quotes History* and *Portfolios*. These tables are accessed, as mentioned earlier, by the system and user transactions. The periodic system transactions update the *Quotes* table, i.e., refreshing the market prices of the stocks. The defined user transactions are four: *VIEW-STOCK, VIEW-PORTFOLIO, PURCHASE*, and *SALE*. The first two are *read-only transactions*; the last two are *write transactions*. Apart from the testbed, [48] also presented a QoS Management technique consisting of three parts: *overload detection, admission control*, and *adaptive updates*. In this section, these three components are described.

2.9.3 Adaptive Update Policy

Another idea presented in [48] is that of an *Adaptive Update Policy (AUP)*. While
the Admission Control deals with user transactions, the adaptive update policy is
used to reduce the workload of the update transactions, as shown in figure 2.21. For
that, the concept of *flexible validity interval* [49] is used to relax the absolute validity
intervals. First, an access update radio is computed:

$$AUR[i] = \frac{AF[i]}{UF[i]} \tag{2.16}$$

where $AF[i]$ is the access frequency of a data item d_i, and $UF[i]$ is the update
frequency of the same data item. $AUR[i]$ measures how hot the data item is. If
$AUR[i] > 1$, the data item d_i is considered hot because that means the data item is
used many times between updates.

Based on the $AUR[i]$ value, a data item can be updated less frequently if considered cold. So, initially, the flexible validity interval is $fvi[i] = avi[i]$. Later on, if
the data item is found to be cold, $fvi[i]$ can be relaxed in the following range:

$$avi[i] \leq fvi[i] \leq \beta \cdot avi[i] \tag{2.17}$$

where β is the *update period relaxation bound*.

The problem is then to find which data items are cold. One option is to sort the
values $AUR[i]$. Kang et al. perform a linear search over an array to avoid periodic
sorting. Once cold data is found, the system checks if it is possible to relax the $fvi[i]$
further within the range described in the equation 2.17. In Chronos, this process is
repeated for $\min(n, \delta_s(k) \cdot n)$ data items.

2.9.4 Experiments in Chronos

Kang et al. performed two experiments in the cited paper. The first one measured the
number of *Timely Transactions per Second* (TTPS) as a function of the number of
threads executing transactions in the system. They compared three sets of numbers.
The first corresponds to their baseline, which consists of running the workload under
Berkeley DB. The second set of numbers corresponds to the experiments using
the admission control policy (AC) described in section 1.6 on top of Berkeley DB.
Finally, the third set of numbers refers to the experiments using AUP with Berkeley
DB.

As expected, Kang et al. found that the number of Timely Transactions per second
decreases when the number of concurrent client threads increases. However, they
also found that, in general, the best success rate is achieved with their Adaptive
Update Policy. Unfortunately, there is no elaboration on the exact TTPS percentage.
So, it is impossible to determine the absolute optimality of the approaches. They
only mention that between 20 and 30 percent of the transactions experience long

transaction delays without further explanation. Another drawback, the authors say, is the large confidence intervals of the AUP experiment.

One more conclusion can be derived from this experiment: admission control (at least as designed in [48]) may be a bad strategy for systems with a moderate workload since it leads to a low success rate for a small number of client threads. This contrasts with [49] and [9]. Finally, although AUP outperforms AC for low workloads, their admission control policy behaves similarly to AUP for high workloads. Other metrics collected in [48] is the *average response time*. They showed that their admission control policy behaves better than the baseline and AUP. However, this may be due to dropping too many transactions, as described before. These results show how the traditional metrics used in conventional database systems are not suitable for measuring the performance of real-time systems.

After the results presented in [48], Kang et al. moved their approach for achieving the desired data service delays to control theory. The results are shown in [46]. In that paper, the QoS Manager illustrated in figure 2.21 is changed to a Feedback Control module as shown in figure 2.22.

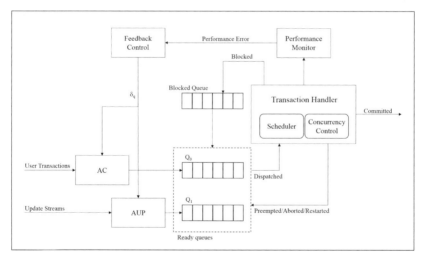

Fig. 2.22 Chronos Architecture

Similar to the previous paper, two proposals are presented: an Admission Control Policy and an Adaptive Update Policy. Both aspects are briefly described next.

They developed the ideas in the paper based on the critical observation that when the system is overloaded, the size of the ready queue increases (see figure 2.22); similarly, when the system is underloaded, the size of the ready queue decreases. So, Kang et al. developed a model for the relation between the ready queue length and the response time. As before, the performance monitor calculates the response time error, and based on this information, the feedback controller computes the required adjustments. The service delay error is obtained as $e(k) = D_s - d(k)$ for the kth sampling period. In this case, D_s is the desired delay, and $d(k)$ is the average response times of the transactions that finished in the sampling interval $[(k-1)SP, kSP]$. Then, the control signal $\delta_q(k)$ is calculated based on $e(k)$. Under overload, $\delta_q(k) < 0$, and some action must be performed to mitigate this situation.

The Adaptive Update Policy establishes one action. The AUP dictates that the period of the cold data must be increased by $(p[i]_{new} - p[i])/p[i]$. By doing this repeatedly, δ_q should become greater than 0. As in the original paper [48], the AUR approach for determining cold/hot data is used. However, in this case, the update period is allowed to increase using the following:

$$p[i]_{new} = \min(\frac{p[i]}{AUR[i]}, P_{max}) \qquad (2.18)$$

In the paper, $P_{max} = 5s$.

Once the new update period is obtained, the flexible validity interval for data item i is changed to $fvi[i]_{new} = 2p[i]$ as in the original paper. The proposed Admission Control Policy establishes the second type of action. When the system is overloaded, the size of the ready queue is modified. According to the AC, the new queue size for the sampling period k is $q(k) = q(k-1) + \delta_q(k)$. The queue size is increased when $\delta_q(k) > 0$ and it is reduced when $\delta_q(k) < 0$. In the research paper, the queue can grow to *max_size*. Beyond this point, incoming transactions are dropped upon arrival.

Now, the question is: How did they obtain $\delta_q(k)$? By applying control theory methods, they developed the Proportional Integral (PI) control law model shown in equation 2.19.

$$q(k) = q(k-1) + K_P[(K_1 + 1)e(k) - e(k-1)] \qquad (2.19)$$

where $K_p = 1.29$ and $K_1 = 2.01$, according to their calculations [46].

Using an implementation of the model in equation 2.19, they performed experiments with similar settings as those in [48]. One modification was the introduction of burst workload to measure how the system adapts to it.

In [46], they performed experiments for four configurations:

1. Pure Berkeley DB implementation
2. Ad-hoc admission control module
3. Pure Feedback Control (FC-C)
4. Feedback Control with Adaptive Updates (FC-CU)

Based on their experiments, Kang et al. concluded that FC-CU was able to reduce the average response time while increasing the percentage of timely transactions. Regarding the latter, one improvement in the report of the experiments is that this time they also showed the total number of transactions.

A critical contribution of the paper is the management of transaction bursts. Kang et al. showed that, in general, the response time is relatively steady for FC-CU in the presence of bursts, with large values only during database initialization and another in the middle experiment. However, an explanation would need to be provided for the former.

In conclusion, [46] shows how control theory can be applied in real-time databases to achieve the desired service delays.

Chapter 3
Commercial Real-Time Database Systems

Commercial real-time database systems refer to database management systems (DBMS) that are developed and offered by commercial vendors as products or services. These systems are designed to meet the requirements of real-time data processing and management in various industries and domains. Unlike experimental systems, commercial real-time database systems are intended for production environments and are backed by professional support, maintenance, and ongoing development.

Commercial real-time database systems provide robust and scalable solutions for handling time-critical data with predictable response times. They offer a wide range of features and functionalities specifically tailored for real-time applications, ensuring efficient data storage, retrieval, and processing. These systems are often designed to handle high volumes of data and simultaneous user interactions while meeting strict timing constraints. Overall, commercial real-time database systems provide powerful and comprehensive solutions for managing and processing real-time data, empowering organizations to derive actionable insights, make informed decisions, and deliver real-time experiences to their users.

This chapter focuses on commercial real-time database systems, exploring their features, capabilities, and applications. The chapter delves into the unique characteristics and functionalities of each system, highlighting their real-time capabilities and supported platforms.

3.1 SQLite Database Management System

SQLite [23] is a software library (See Figure 3.1) that provides a self-contained, serverless, zero-configuration, transactional SQL database engine. Uniquely, SQLite does not require a separate server process or system to operate, and it is devoid of any external dependencies. This makes SQLite an embedded database, meaning that it is used for local/client storage within the end program, as opposed to a standalone database server.

© The Author(s), under exclusive license to Springer Nature Switzerland AG 2024
P. Mejia Alvarez et al., *Real-Time Database Systems*, SpringerBriefs in Computer Science,
https://doi.org/10.1007/978-3-031-44230-8_3

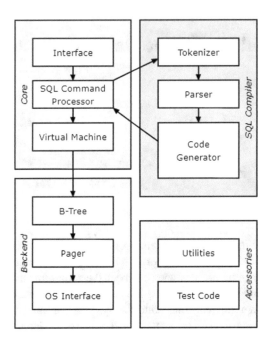

Fig. 3.1 SQLite Architecture

SQLite is a C-language library that implements a small, fast, self-contained, high-reliability, full-featured SQL database engine. SQLite is a relational database management system. In contrast to many other database management systems, SQLite is not a client-server database engine. Instead, it is embedded into the end program. As a result, SQLite is the most used database engine in the world. It is built into all mobile phones and most computers and comes bundled with countless other applications that people use daily. SQLite is ACID-compliant and implements most SQL standards, generally following PostgreSQL syntax. However, SQLite uses a dynamically and weakly typed SQL syntax that does not guarantee domain integrity. This means that one can, for example, insert a string into a column defined as an integer. SQLite will attempt to convert data between formats where appropriate.

SQLite is a good fit for embedded devices, particularly for resource-constrained IoT devices. It has a small code footprint, uses memory and disk space efficiently, is reliable, and requires little maintenance. In addition, because it comes with a command line interface, it can be used to analyze large datasets. Finally, even in enterprises, SQLite can stand in for traditional databases for testing, prototyping, or as a local cache that can make the application more resilient to network outages.

Applications can use SQLite instead of file access commands such as fopen, fread, and fwrite. These commands are often used to manage various file formats such as XML, JSON, or CSV, and there's a need to write parsers for these. SQLite removes this extra work. In addition, because SQLite packs data efficiently, it's faster than these commands. It's been noted that.

3.1.1 SQLite in RTOS Environments

SQLite's compact and self-sustained nature makes it a perfect match for RTOS environments. In addition, the database engine's small footprint means it demands minimal resources, a critical feature for RTOS environments where system resources are often constrained. SQLite has been designed to be embedded into other applications, making it a prevalent choice for embedded systems, including those running on RTOS. In addition, SQLite's footprint, which is around 600KiB or less with all features enabled, and its serverless architecture make it ideally suited for use in RTOS environments that often have limited storage and processing capabilities. Moreover, SQLite is self-contained, which means it requires minimal support from external libraries or the operating system, and it can function across different operating system platforms without requiring any modifications. This makes it easy to incorporate SQLite into a variety of RTOS environments. SQLite also provides a simple, easy-to-use API and supports a wide range of SQL syntax, making it a versatile choice for embedded database solutions.

SQLite, being a self-contained, serverless, and zero-configuration database engine, is compatible with a broad range of Real-Time Operating Systems (RTOS). Here, we will explore a few more examples in detail:

- **RTEMS**: RTEMS (Real-Time Executive for Multiprocessor Systems) is a free open-source RTOS designed for real-time applications within embedded systems. Known for its high configurability, it provides a robust environment for SQLite to operate on, especially in multiprocessor systems.
- **eCos**: The Embedded Configurable Operating System (eCos) is a free and open-source RTOS intended for real-time embedded systems. As a configurable and adaptable system, eCos allows developers to tailor it for specific applications, which can be beneficial when integrating SQLite.
- **VxWorks** VxWorks by Wind River is a widely used RTOS that is designed to be robust, scalable, and suitable for use in safety-critical applications. In addition, SQLite can be integrated into VxWorks to provide a reliable and efficient database solution for embedded applications.
- **QNX**: QNX is a commercial Unix-like real-time operating system aimed primarily at the embedded systems market. It provides a highly reliable environment where SQLite can operate efficiently, providing database services to applications.
- **µC/OS**: µC/OS is a scalable and ROMable RTOS that is known for its small footprint and deterministic behavior. SQLite's ability to manage data efficiently can greatly benefit such environments, especially when operating on devices with limited storage and processing capabilities.

While these are just a few examples, SQLite can be integrated with almost any RTOS or general-purpose OS that provides basic POSIX-like file system capabilities. This adaptability is one of the reasons SQLite is a popular choice for embedded database solutions.

3.2 ITTIA DB: Time Series Platform for Building Embedded Systems and IoT Devices

ITTIA DB is an embeddable data management and analytics software platform for streaming, analytics, and data management on edge devices. Application software built for MCUs, MPUs, and ECUs is tightly integrated with ITTIA DB, which is silently embedded and does not need an administrator.

Specially designed for hybrid transaction/analytical processing (HTAP) queries, ITTIA DB combines real-time stream processing with high-performance time series and table data storage. HTAP is an emerging application architecture that "breaks the wall" between reliable transaction processing and analytics for real-time decision-making. ITTIA DB brings HTAP capability to embedded systems and IoT devices. Developers of embedded systems and IoT device applications choose ITTIA DB to collect, process, and analyze incoming data point streams in real-time. As a time series database, ITTIA DB is architected to record and search time-stamped values efficiently. With real-time stream processing, measurements and events produced by sensors and IoT nodes are easily downsampled, filtered, and aggregated over a desired time period. Results are recorded as compressed time series data sets that can be searched, summarized, or transmitted to other devices and services.

Modern domain-specific embedded systems (e.g., automotive, aerospace, industrial control, defense, medical devices, etc.) run safety-critical applications for which database failure or data loss may result in a catastrophic event. Such systems avoid general-purpose embedded databases and leverage ITTIA DB in mission-critical environments. Moreover, many of these systems operate over networks that make them susceptible to various attacks. Hence, the reliability, safety, and security of embedded systems incorporating ITTIA DB are very important.

ITTIA security practices and features assist manufacturers of IoT edge devices with advanced and integrated software development methods infused by a secure development life cycle (SDL) based on zero trust principles, enabling makers of IoT edge devices to mitigate unpredictability. From product conception to end-of-life, ITTIA adheres to a secure-by-design development methodology, and ITTIA DB offers a complete solution to secure data on IoT devices. Furthermore, ITTIA SDL Is Conformant to the Principles of IEC/ISO 62443. ITTIA DB also offers software solutions for Disaster Recovery (DR) and High Availability (HA) on the microcontroller, microprocessor, and electronic control unit devices that leverage redundant storage media, sensors, devices, and networks to increase uptime for data stored on the IoT edge. For example, devices that are individually only 98% reliable can offer over 99.9% uptime when connected by ITTIA DB.

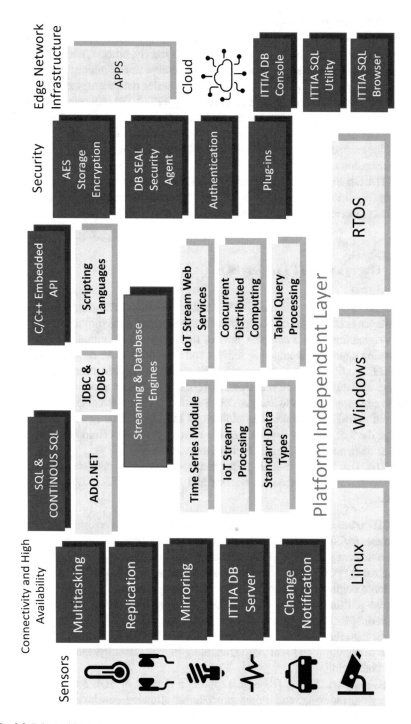

Fig. 3.2 Ittia Architecture

ITTIA DB SQL is a high-performance time-series embedded database for single or multicore microprocessors (MPUs) and Electronic Control Units (ECUs) that enable manufacturers to build systems to monitor securely, process, and store real-time data. This secure embedded database for edge computing combines powerful capabilities, such as real-time data streaming, time series data management, high-level security, high availability, and disaster recovery. ITTIA DB SQL empowers devices to overcome latency and bandwidth performance constraints. From the ground up, ITTIA DB SQL is architected to provide database capabilities to application developers for embedded systems and devices without requiring complex installation or administration tools.

ITTIA DB SQL data management capabilities offer benefits in its modular architecture (Figure 3.2 that enables developers to create highly optimized and reliable systems to store, manage, and distribute data.

3.2.1 Overview of ITTIA DB SQL

ITTIA DB SQL offers efficient filtering and processing of real-time data. One of its advantages is integrated device stream data processing, which filters and processes data originating from a complex flow of data events. In addition, its special data processing capabilities empower sensors and devices to make sense of every bit of raw data, identify alarming events, and store meaningful information. With a massive volume of data flowing in real-time, ITTIA DB SQL data processing capabilities enable edge applications to analyze data, perform continuous real-time SQL queries, and configure data distribution. In addition, ITTIA DB SQL is scalable to any number of edge devices, so edge applications can capture data flows from multiple sources, analyze data, and emit valuable findings as events.

ITTIA DB SQL is a high-performance, lightweight, and scalable relational database that targets embedded systems and IoT devices. Some of its key features include:

- **ACID transactions**: ITTIA DB SQL supports atomic, consistent, isolated, and durable (ACID) transactions to ensure data integrity and consistency.
- **Concurrency control**: ITTIA DB SQL implements multi-version concurrency control (MVCC) to allow multiple transactions to be processed simultaneously without conflicts or delays.
- **Cross-platform support**: ITTIA DB SQL can be used on various platforms, including Windows, Linux, Android, and many embedded operating systems.
- **Data distribution and replication**: ITTIA DB SQL provides mechanisms for data distribution and replication, enabling high availability, fault tolerance, and load balancing.
- **SQL support**: ITTIA DB SQL supports a rich set of SQL features, including querying, indexing, and stored procedures, allowing developers to work with familiar SQL syntax.

- **Time Series Platform**: ITTIA DB SQL is architected and built as time series software optimized for storing and serving time series through associated pairs of timestamps and values. When you embed ITTIA DB SQL, sensors, devices, and IoT nodes that produce timestamped data points can down-sample, filter, and aggregate large volumes of data in real-time. ITTIA DB SQL is designed to process and store an embedded system's data efficiently, simultaneously capturing information and discarding irrelevant data.
- **High Availability & Disaster Recovery**: ITTIA DB SQL's current high availability protects the embedded system from losing data and offers manufacturers a way to avoid lost revenue when access to data is disrupted. In addition, high availability, fault tolerance, planned and unplanned interruption, disaster recovery, balance loading, and database backup offer the peace of mind embedded system builders desire to stay competitive.
- **Safety, Security, Certifiability**: Modern domain-specific embedded systems (e.g., automotive, aerospace, industrial control, defense, medical devices, etc.) run safety-critical applications for which database failure or data loss may result in a catastrophic event. Such systems avoid general-purpose embedded databases and leverage ITTIA DB SQL in mission-critical environments. Moreover, many of these systems operate over networks, making them susceptible to various attacks. Hence, the reliability, safety, security, and certifiability of embedded systems incorporating ITTIA DB SQL are very important.
- **Hard Real-Time & Small Footprint**: ITTIA DB SQL utilizes hard real-time processing to handle workloads in a constantly changing state. It is a scalable edge database that dramatically simplifies building real-time applications for embedded systems. ITTIA DB SQL provides a very low latency data management platform that enables real-time event processing, data movement, and analytics ideal for edge computing.

3.2.2 Supported 3rd Party Platforms

The following third-party tools are tested, supported, and recommended for integration with ITTIA DB SQL. Our goal is to offer customers access to qualified technologies, already verified with our database software, that will save time and cost.

1. **Development Suites and Compilers**: IAR Embedded Workbench, GNU Compiler Collection, Green Hills Software MULTI Integrated Development Environment, Microsoft Visual Studio
2. **Embedded Operating Systems** ITTIA databases support various Embedded Operating Systems, including Green Hills Software INTEGRITY RTOS Family, Micrium RTOS Kernels, QNX Neutrino, Wind River VxWorks, Azure RTOS ThreadX, FreeRTOS, Linux, Android, and others.
3. **Connectivity and Data Distribution**, with support from RTI Connext DDS and others.

4. **Graphical User Interfaces** ITTIA databases support various Graphical User Interfaces, including Crank Software Storyboard Suite, Qt, and others.
5. **Variety of Processors & Boards**: ITTIA databases support various hardware architectures, including Arm, Intel, and PowerPC. With support for industry-leading commercial off-the-shelf (COTS) Board Support Packages (BSP), ITTIA DB SQL builds and supports different package requirements. In addition, ITTIA DB SQL is cross-platform and supports processor families from leading manufacturers, including AMD, ARM, Broadcom, Intel, NXP, Renesas, STMicroelectronics, Texas Instruments, Xilinx, NXP, Cypress, Microchip, Texas Instruments, and others.
6. **Computers on Module** ITTIA databases support various Computer on Modules, including Toradex, TQ Group, PHYTEC, iWave, and others.

3.2.3 Real-Time Features

When integrated with an RTOS, ITTIA DB SQL can take advantage of the RTOS's real-time capabilities, such as:

- **Deterministic Scheduling**: RTOS provides deterministic scheduling algorithms, like rate-monotonic or earliest deadline first scheduling, ensuring tasks are executed in a predictable and timely manner.
- **Priority-Based Task Management**: RTOS enables priority-based task management, prioritizing critical tasks over less critical tasks.
- **Inter-Process Communication**: RTOS facilitates efficient inter-process communication, allowing tasks to share data, synchronize, and coordinate their execution.
- **Memory Management**: RTOS provides memory management mechanisms, ensuring efficient use of memory resources and preventing memory leaks or fragmentation.

3.3 Raima Database Manager (RDM)

Raima Database Manager (RDM) [70] is an ACID-compliant embedded database management system designed for use in embedded systems applications (See Figure 3.3). RDM has been designed to utilize multi-core computers, networking (local or wide area), and on-disk or in-memory storage management. RDM provides support for multiple application programming interfaces (APIs): low-level C API, C++, and SQL (native, ODBC, JDBC, ADO.NET, and REST). RDM is highly portable and is available on Windows, Linux, Unix, and several real-time or embedded operating systems. A source-code license is also available.

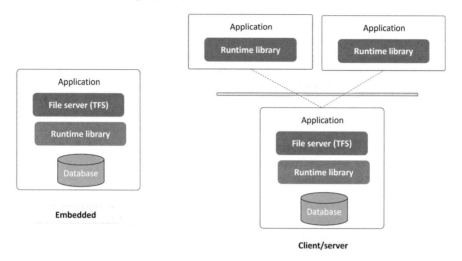

Fig. 3.3 RAIMA Architecture

3.3.1 Non-SQL and SQL Database Design and Manipulation

RDM has support for both non-SQL (record and cursor level database access) and SQL database design and manipulation capabilities. The non-SQL features are important for the most resource-restricted embedded system environments, where high performance in a small footprint is the priority. SQL is essential in providing a widely known standard database access method in a small enough footprint for most embedded systems environments. Raima Inc. originally released RDM in 1984, and it was called db_VISTA. It was one of the first microcomputer network model database management systems designed exclusively for use with C language applications. A companion product called db_QUERY was introduced in 1986, which was the first SQL-like query and report-writing utility for a network model database.

3.3.2 Product Features

Both the source code lines and features in Raima Database Manager and RDM Server are consolidated into one source code. RDM includes these major features: updated in-memory support, time series and FFT support, snapshots, R-Tree support, compression, encryption, SQL, SQL PL, and platform independence—develop once, deploy anywhere. RMD includes portability options such as direct copy and pastes that permit development and deployment on different target platforms, regardless of architecture or byte order. The release consists of a streamlined interface that is cursor-based, extended SQL support, and stored procedures that support SQL PL; it also supports ODBC (C, $C++$), ADO.NET ($C\#$), RESTful, and JDBC (Java). Supported development environments include Microsoft Visual Studio, Apple XCode, Eclipse, and Wind River Workbench. A redesigned and optimized database file format architecture maintains ACID compliance and data safeguards, with different formats for in-memory, on-disk, or hybrid storage. In addition, file formats hide hardware platform specifics (e.g., byte ordering). Download packages include examples of RDM speed and performance benchmarks.

Raima has three modes of operation:

1. Single-Process, Multi-Thread
2. Multi-Process, separate Transactional File Server
3. Multi-Process, shared in-process Transactional File Server

Raima support for on-the-fly alterations of the database and tables themselves (Dynamic DDL) and support the encryption of AES 128, 192, 256 bit.

Data Providers and Drivers for Interoperability in Raima are:

- ADO.Net 4.0 Data Provider
- JDBC 4.2 Type 4 Driver
- ODBC 3.51 Driver
- RESTful API

Also, Raima provides the following different "tree" support:

- AVL-Tree Indexing support
- B-Tree indexing support
- R-Tree indexing support
- Hash table indexing support

3.3.3 Transactional File Server (TFS)

A software component within the RDM system that maintains safe multi-user transactional updates to a set of files and responds to page requests. The TFServer utility links to the TFS to allow it to run as a separate utility, allowing users to run RDM in a distributed computing environment. The TFS may also be linked directly to an application to avoid the RPC overhead of calling a separate server.

3.3.4 Snapshots

Snapshot isolation allows concurrent reads to the database when write transactions are occurring. RDM takes a frozen image of the system's current state, and that information can be read without stopping writing. At any point, the user can issue a snapshot of specific tables by calling our rdm_dbStartSnapshot() API. Once done, the RDM system will create a static view of the tables specified, where any changes to those tables will not be reflected in the snapshot. The user is then free to issue writes to that table outside the snapshot, and any reads within the snapshot view will not be waiting for those writes to complete or preventing those writes from finishing. Once the snapshot is no longer needed, a simple end transaction can be called to easily and quickly get rid of it. This feature provides the end user with the largest number of writes and reads possible simultaneously.

3.3.5 Circular Tables support

A record type, or table, can be defined as "circular." With circular tables, RDM will still allow new record instances to be created when the table becomes full. However, the new record instances will overwrite existing ones, starting with the oldest. RDM does not allow explicitly deleting record instances in a circular table. The definition of a circular table includes a size limit. This provides a valuable way of allocating a fixed amount of storage space for storing the most recent instances of a particular record type. For example, this may be useful in storing event data generated rapidly, where only the most recent data is relevant. In addition, circular tables remove the risk that incoming data may fail to be stored due to a lack of space while avoiding the need for the application to delete obsolete data.

3.4 eXtremeDB-RT

Time is of the essence for mission and safety-critical systems software in avionics, autonomous systems, railroad, critical control systems, and the like. Consequently, these systems demand deterministic, predictable, fully controllable database management that complements modern real-time operating systems' time and space partitioning and advanced real-time schedulers. Often non-interruptible and with stringent requirements on timely execution, these systems' data management imposes temporal constraints on critical data and transactions.

eXtremeDB/rt [28] is the first of its kind commercial, supported database management system designed to preserve the temporal validity of data through time-cognizant transaction processing that guarantees the predictable execution of transactions. In simpler terms, eXtremeDB/rt is a deterministic, hard real-time database system. eXtremeDB/rt extends conventional eXtremeDB transaction processing by adding semantics for, and enforcing, database transaction priorities and deadline scheduling. Like conventional eXtremeDB, eXtremeDB/rt is an embedded database management system that provides services for storing, retrieving, and manipulating data. The differences lay in the temporal requirements of the managed data, transaction scheduling policies, timing constraints on transactions, and performance goals. Conventional eXtremeDB, like other ACID-compliant DBMSs, maintains the internal consistency of databases, preventing contradictory data in the same database. In addition to preserving internal consistency, eXtremeDB/rt safeguards the temporal consistency of data. The eXtremeDB/rt kernel exposes transaction deadline semantics through a real-time transaction manager that ensures that transactions can meet (successfully commit) or *miss* (successfully abort) their deadlines but can never be late (run past their deadline) to commit or abort.

The eXtremeDB/rt kernel modifies the conventional eXtremeDB kernel by ensuring that all database kernel components are time-cognizant. The eXtremeDB/rt transaction scheduler offers a High Priority Earliest Deadline First (EDF) algorithm: transactions are scheduled for execution based on their priority and deadline, and a Priority Inheritance (PI) algorithm. The deadlines are enforced through a sophisticated rollback mechanism that allows transactions to modify or retrieve data only if they can complete within the set deadlines. The database kernel identifies transactions destined to be late, interrupts them, and forces the rollback in time to satisfy the deadlines.

3.4.1 Temporal Consistency

One of the most important differences between the database systems used by real-time and non-real-time systems is that while a conventional (non-real-time) DBMS aims to achieve good throughput or average response time and maintains logical *internal* consistency, a real-time DBMS must maintain temporal *external* consistency as well as providing predictable response time and guaranteeing the completion of time-critical transactions and making sure that data used by them reflects the current physical environment. Therefore, the design of a real-time database system should avoid using techniques that introduce unpredictable latencies. Meeting all deadlines requested by all system events is vital to real-time systems. To achieve its goal of guaranteed transaction commit or rollback times, the eXtremeDB/rt database runtime relies upon the following assertion: *The time required to reverse any modifications to the database made by a transaction up to any point in the transaction does not exceed the time required to apply those modifications.*

3.4.2 RT Transaction Scheduling

Scheduling transactions in a real-time database system is not a simple task. The database must guarantee the database's logical consistency and schedule transactions to meet their deadlines while minimizing the number of transactions that miss their deadlines. Several scheduling policies use different criteria to prioritize transactions.

We provide two alternative implementations:

- **High Priority Earliest Deadline First (EDF) algorithm**: transactions are sorted in the queue based first on their priority and then within the same priority - by the deadline. The corresponding transaction manager is based on MURSIW.

- **Priority Inheritance (PI) algorithm**: the transaction manager (PI-TM) relies on the real-time operating system's (RTOS) scheduling and provides necessary hints via specific usage of OS synchronization primitives. A fixed-size set of synchronization primitives is allocated when a database is created. These synchronization primitives are used as mutexes: Upon the start of a transaction, the thread grabs one or more mutex (one for a Read-Only transaction, chosen randomly; all mutexes for a Read-Write transaction, in the order that prevents deadlocks) and releases them when the transaction ends. Thus, the OS scheduler is fully aware of which thread holds a mutex that is needed for a high-priority transaction and may apply *priority inheritance* when required and if available (for example: in Linux and $FreeRTOS^{TM}$), i.e., temporarily raise the priority of a thread that is in the way to let it finish the transaction faster so it can release the highly needed *mutex*.

The number of synchronization primitives is set by a database parameter that defines the maximum number of Read-Only transactions running in parallel. This parameter is called *mco_db_params_t.max_pi_readers*. The default value is 1, meaning that PI-TM will behave as EXCL (mcotexcl).

PI-TM (mcotmpi) is available on Linux, LynxOS-178®, FreeRTOS, embOS, $INTEGRITY^{TM}$, and $VxWorks^{TM}$.

Once scheduled, a transaction's execution is controlled by the transaction manager that ensures proper serialization (*read-write* transactions are executed sequentially, *read-only* transactions are executed in parallel while no *read-write* transactions are running)

The preemption rules are as follows:

- A higher priority Read-Write transaction preempts all running lower priority Read-Only transactions (causing them to rollback, first) unless there is also a running Read-Only transaction with even higher priority than this read-write transaction has. In this case, the Read-Write transaction will be placed at the appropriate location in the queue according to its priority and deadline. [Note: With PI-TM, if the higher priority Read-Only transaction completes before, the lower priority Read-Only transactions that are executing in parallel, the higher priority Read-Write transaction will preempt the remaining Read-Only transactions. With MURSIW, once a transaction is placed in the queue, it will just wait its turn.]
- A higher priority Read-Only or Read-Write transaction preempts a lower priority Read-Write transaction (causing it to rollback, first) if the elapsed running time (and, consequently, the time of termination via rollback) of the running transaction is less than the new transaction's deadline. In other words, if the time required to preempt the running transaction, including rolling it back, would preclude the higher priority transaction from being able to commit before its deadline, then the currently running transaction will not be preempted because the result would be two rolled-back transactions.

The eXtremeDB/rt transaction manager has many verification checkpoints at which a transaction's elapsed time is tested against the deadline. The frequency of the verifications eliminates the possibility of going beyond the set deadline. If the control point is reached (the transaction used up the allotted time slice), the transaction is assigned a unique *transaction interrupted* status. ($MCO\_E\_INTERRUPTED$), and the control is returned to the application. The application is then expected to rollback the transaction. The transaction manager ensures that all database runtime internals is in a *recoverable* condition and that a subsequent transaction rollback will restore the database to a consistent state before the transaction starts. Furthermore, the transaction manager guarantees that the rollback is completed within the deadline, provided that the application initiates the rollback when signaled to do so by the database runtime. Thus, the transaction would miss the deadline but not be *late*, and the internal consistency of the database is preserved.

EDF vs PI-TM

PI-TM is advantageous in the situation with a high-priority thread (let's call it H_DB) that performs transactions with the database, a low-priority thread that also performs transactions (L_DB) and a mid-priority thread that does not work with the database (M).

Let's consider the following scenario. L_DB starts a transaction. Subsequently, M comes in and (having a higher priority) preempts the L_DB, taking it *off the CPU* and putting it on hold. Next, H_DB arrives but cannot start a transaction because L_DB is in the way. Essentially, with EDF, the highest priority thread H_DB will have to wait until the lowest priority thread L_DB completes its transaction. However, with PI_TM the operating system will be able to raise $L\_DB's$ priority up to $H\_DB's$ priority at the moment when H_DB arrives, allowing L_DB to preempt M, allowing L_DB to complete its transaction and free the way for H_DB.

The following heuristics should be taken into consideration for PI-TM used for CPU-intensive transactions:

- The number of initially allocated synchronization primitives should be the same as the number of CPU cores. (It does not make much sense to allow more Read-Only transactions than can be run simultaneously using different cores, as this would make each transaction longer.)
- The greater the number of allocated PI-TM synchronization primitives, the harder it is to start a Read-Write transaction (the Read-Write transaction potentially must wait until every competing Read-Only transaction releases its primitive). Therefore, in practice, the PI-TM applies to hardware configurations with 1-4 CPU cores.

3.4.3 Methods to Enforce Deadlines

The key to supporting real-time transactions is the ability of the database runtime to interrupt the execution of the current transaction safely. Two methods are available: through an asynchronous event handler or via an application callback that is passed to the database runtime and is invoked periodically during a transaction, signaling the application that the deadline control point was reached.

1. **The Callback Method**: This method is usually employed when asynchronous primitives such as a system timer or a hardware watchdog are unavailable. For example, the application often polls a system clock or responds to hardware interrupts, etc. To use a callback, the application registers a callback function with the database runtime. The eXtremeDB runtime provides a standard method for registering various callbacks.

2. **The Timer Method**: The first step in using the timer-based transaction control method is determining the transaction control point. As discussed, setting the control point to half of the deadline interval is often safe (as discussed earlier, this measure could be too rough and hurt the miss/meet deadline ratio). Then the application starts the timer, setting the timer period to the control point determined in the first step. Installing a timer is operating system-specific and is not complicated.

3.4.4 Supported platforms

Real-time applications must run in the context of a real-time operating system or be able to access hardware resources — interrupts, timers, memory management, etc. eXtremeDB/rt is currently available for the following real-time operating systems on selected hardware platforms (the list of platforms is constantly expanding).

- Deos™, (native and ARINC 653-compliant) from DDC-I
- FreeRTOS™, a widely used real-time operating system kernel for embedded devices
- INTEGRITY® from Green Hills Software
- LynxOS-178® from Lynx Software Technologies, a hard real-time partitioning operating system developed and certified to FAA DO-178B/C DAL A safety standards
- VxWorks® 6.9, 7.0, and 653 from WindRiver
- embOS
- PetaLinux
- Nucleus™
- Azure RTOS ThreadX
- MICROSAR

Chapter 4
Applications of Real-Time Database Systems

In previous chapters, we briefly described a few examples of the applicability of real-time database systems. However, it is worth explaining other scenarios where they are used so that we can get a better grasp of how important this area is. Recently, there has been a trend toward applying the results of this core RTDB research to other related applications. The key ingredients of these applications are the requirements for real-time response to requests for real-time data.

Real-time database management systems (RTDBMS) are designed to handle applications that require fast and deterministic response times, data consistency, and time-constrained data processing. This chapter introduces some typical critical applications for real-time database management systems. These are just a few examples of the many applications where real-time database management systems can be beneficial. The primary advantage of using an RTDBMS is its ability to handle time-sensitive data processing and decision-making, ensuring data consistency and deterministic response times. This chapter explores the wide range of applications where real-time databases play a crucial role in managing and processing time-sensitive data. It highlights the significance of real-time databases in various industries and domains, showcasing their practical applications and benefits. The chapter delves into specific use cases and examples, demonstrating how real-time databases enable efficient data management, analysis, and decision-making in time-critical scenarios.

By the end of this chapter, readers will have gained a comprehensive understanding of the practical applications of real-time databases across various industries. They will recognize the significance of real-time data management in different domains and appreciate how real-time databases enable efficient data processing, analysis, and decision-making in time-critical scenarios. This knowledge will help readers identify potential use cases and opportunities for implementing real-time database systems in their respective fields.

© The Author(s), under exclusive license to Springer Nature Switzerland AG 2024
P. Mejia Alvarez et al., *Real-Time Database Systems*, SpringerBriefs in Computer Science,
https://doi.org/10.1007/978-3-031-44230-8_4

4.1 Military Command and Control Systems (MCCS)

MCCS is essential for managing and coordinating military assets, personnel, and information in a complex and rapidly changing operational environment. Real-time responses and efficient database management systems are crucial to the effective functioning of MCCS, enabling military commanders to make informed decisions quickly and maintain situational awareness. Here is a more detailed overview of real-time responses and database management systems in MCCS [8]:

1. **Real-time Data Fusion**: must integrate data from multiple sources, including intelligence, surveillance, reconnaissance (ISR) assets, communication networks, sensors, and other systems. This data fusion gives commanders a comprehensive and up-to-date situational picture, allowing them to understand the operational environment and make informed decisions. Real-time data processing techniques, such as sensor fusion algorithms and artificial intelligence, help aggregate and synthesize this data.

2. **Real-time Command and Control**: facilitate real-time command and control by enabling commanders to issue orders and directives to subordinate units, monitor their progress, and receive updates on their status. Real-time communication channels and collaboration tools, such as chat, voice, and video, allow commanders to maintain constant contact with their units and coordinate their actions effectively.

3. **Real-time Decision Support Tools**: Advanced decision support tools integrated into MCCS help commanders analyze the operational environment, assess risks, and identify optimal courses of action. These tools may incorporate artificial intelligence, machine learning, and predictive analytics to process real-time data and provide insights, alerts, and recommendations. Such tools can support decision-making at various levels, from tactical to strategic.

4. **Real-time Situational Awareness**: provides real-time situational awareness by displaying the current positions, statuses, and activities of friendly and enemy forces, as well as relevant environmental and contextual information. Geographic information systems (GIS) and other visualization tools enable commanders to view this information in an intuitive and easily understandable format.

5. **Real-time Resource Tracking and Management**: MCCS databases track the status, location, and availability of military resources, including personnel, vehicles, weapons, and supplies. Real-time resource management tools help commanders allocate and deploy these resources efficiently in response to changing operational requirements.

6. **Real-time Intelligence Processing and Dissemination**: manage and process intelligence data from various sources, such as imagery, signals intelligence (SIGINT), and human intelligence (HUMINT). Database management systems must be designed to efficiently store, organize, and retrieve this data, allowing commanders and intelligence analysts to access and analyze it in real-time. The timely dissemination of intelligence is crucial for maintaining situational awareness and making informed decisions.

7. **Cybersecurity and Information Assurance**: MCCS must ensure the security, integrity, and availability of the data they process and store. This involves implementing robust cybersecurity measures, such as encryption, authentication, and intrusion detection systems, to protect sensitive information and ensure the continuity of command and control functions in the face of cyber threats.

8. **Scalability, Performance, and Resilience**: MCCS databases must be scalable and capable of handling the increasing volume of data generated by growing military operations and the continuous evolution of ISR and communication technologies. In addition, database management systems must be optimized for high-performance, low-latency access, and resilience to support real-time military command and control decision-making.

9. **Unmanned Aerial Vehicles (UAVs) and Drones** are crucial for controlling and coordinating UAVs and drones. These systems handle real-time navigation, communication, and payload management data, ensuring that UAVs and drones can complete their missions efficiently and safely.

10. **Missile Defense Systems**: are used to manage and coordinate missile defense systems, ensuring that incoming threats are detected and neutralized in a timely manner. These systems process real-time data related to threat detection, tracking, and countermeasures, allowing for swift and effective decision-making.

11. **Advanced Avionics Systems**: play a critical role in modern avionics systems, ensuring that aircraft can perform complex maneuvers, maintain precise positioning, and communicate effectively with ground control. These systems enable pilots to execute their missions safely and efficiently by processing real-time data.

12. **Space Exploration and Missions**: manage and coordinate various aspects of space exploration missions, including spacecraft navigation, communication, and payload management. These systems ensure that mission-critical tasks are executed promptly and accurately, contributing to the mission's overall success.

In summary, real-time responses and efficient database management systems are vital components of modern Military Command and Control Systems. These capabilities enable commanders to maintain situational awareness, make time-sensitive decisions, and ensure effective communication and coordination between military units and assets in a complex and rapidly changing operational environment.

4.2 Energy and Utilities

Real-time scheduling database management systems (RTDBMS) have numerous applications in the energy and utilities industry. These systems help utility providers to optimize their operations, reduce costs, and improve the reliability of their networks. In this section, we will discuss in more detail some of the primary applications of RTDBMS in the energy and utilities industry [68].

1. **Energy Distribution**: RTDBMS can be used to optimize energy distribution in real-time. By collecting data on energy demand, supply, and other critical factors,

these systems can help utility providers to adjust energy supply and demand to match real-time needs. As a result, real-time energy distribution can help to reduce energy waste, improve network efficiency, and enhance the reliability of energy supply. For example, RTS-DBMS can be used to predict peak demand and adjust energy supply accordingly to reduce the risk of blackouts or brownouts.

2. **Asset Management**: RTDBMS can also be used for real-time asset management in the energy and utilities industry. These systems can collect data on asset performance, maintenance requirements, and other factors, allowing utility providers to optimize asset utilization and reduce maintenance costs. Real-time asset management can also help to identify potential asset failures before they occur, reducing the risk of outages and other service interruptions. For example, RTS-DBMS can monitor the performance of power transformers and alert operators to potential issues before they cause an outage.

3. **Outage Management**: RTDBMS can manage power outages in real-time. By collecting data on outage locations, affected customers, and other critical information, these systems can help utility providers to respond quickly to outages and minimize the duration of service interruptions. Real-time outage management can also help to optimize the allocation of repair crews and other resources, reducing costs and improving service reliability. For example, RTDBMS can prioritize outage restoration based on the number of affected customers and the estimated time to restore service.

4. **Demand Response**: RTDBMS can be used for real-time demand response in the energy and utilities industry. By collecting data on energy demand, utility providers can adjust energy supply and demand to match real-time needs, reducing energy waste and improving network efficiency. Real-time demand response can also help to reduce peak demand, which can help to reduce energy costs for consumers. For example, RTS-DBMS can automatically adjust the temperature set-points in commercial buildings during periods of high demand to reduce energy consumption.

5. **Resource Optimization**: RTDBMS can be used to optimize resource utilization in the energy and utilities industry. Real-time data on energy supply, demand, and other critical factors can be used to allocate resources more efficiently, reducing costs and improving network reliability. For example, RTDBMS can optimize the dispatch of power generation sources to meet real-time demand, reducing the need for expensive peaking power plants.

6. **Customer Service**: RTDBMS can improve customer service in the energy and utilities industry. For example, utility providers can improve transparency and build customer trust by providing real-time updates on outages, service interruptions, and other critical information. Real-time data can also be used to identify and address potential issues before they become a problem, improving the overall customer experience. For example, RTDBMS can be used to automatically send outage notifications to customers via text message or email.

7. **Regulatory Compliance**: RTDBMS can help utility providers to comply with regulatory requirements in the energy and utilities industry. Real-time data on network performance, energy consumption, and other critical factors can be used

to monitor compliance with regulations and quality standards, such as the North American Electric Reliability Corporation (NERC) reliability standards. For example, RTS-DBMS can be used to monitor the frequency and voltage of the electric grid to ensure that it meets regulatory requirements.

8. **Renewable Energy Integration**: RTDBMS can be used to optimize the integration of renewable energy sources into the electric grid. Real-time data on renewable energy generation, energy demand, and other critical factors can balance supply and demand in real-time, ensuring that renewable energy sources are used efficiently and effectively. As a result, real-time renewable energy integration can help to reduce the use of fossil fuels and improve the sustainability of the electric grid.

9. **Cybersecurity**: RTDBMS can be used to enhance cybersecurity in the energy and utilities industry. Real-time data on network traffic and other critical indicators can be used to detect and respond to cybersecurity threats in real-time, reducing the risk of service interruptions and other security breaches. RTS-DBMS can also monitor access to critical infrastructure and identify potential security vulnerabilities before attackers can exploit them.

10. **Predictive Maintenance**: RTDBMS can be used for predictive maintenance in the energy and utilities industry. Real-time data on asset performance and maintenance requirements can predict when maintenance is required and optimize maintenance schedules, reducing costs and improving network reliability. Predictive maintenance can also help to identify potential asset failures before they occur, reducing the risk of outages and other service interruptions.

4.3 Online Gaming

Multiplayer online games and virtual environments require real-time databases to manage and process player actions, game states, and other time-sensitive data [86].

Online gaming is an industry that has been growing exponentially over the past few years, with millions of users playing games simultaneously across the world. To provide a seamless gaming experience, real-time scheduling and database management systems are essential. These systems help manage the complex interactions between players, game servers, and databases, ensuring that the game runs smoothly and without any hiccups.

Several issues in Online Gaming for real-time databases have been studied:

1. **Scheduling**: Real-time scheduling systems are used in online gaming to manage the allocation of server resources and prioritize incoming requests based on the server's current load. This ensures that players can connect to game servers quickly and efficiently, reducing lag or gameplay delays. In addition, real-time scheduling systems manage the availability of resources, including bandwidth, CPU, and memory, ensuring that all players have the same experience and that gameplay remains stable and consistent.

These systems must also provide high throughput, low latency, and reliability, even with large numbers of players. Mobile gaming databases store game states, player information, inventory, and game items, among other data. They are designed to handle a large volume of data, providing quick and reliable data access to players.

2. **Storage of data**: Database management systems are also critical in online gaming, as they store all of the game's data, including player information, game state, and items. These databases must be able to handle large volumes of data while ensuring that the data is consistent and reliable. This is especially important in online gaming,'where multiple players simultaneously interact with the same data.

3. Massive multiplayers: One of the most common applications of real-time scheduling and database management systems in online gaming is in massively multiplayer online role-playing games (MMORPGs). In these games, players interact with each other in a shared virtual world. Real-time scheduling systems manage the allocation of server resources, ensuring that all players can connect to the game and play together. Database management systems store character information, inventory, and quest progress, which different players access simultaneously.

4. **Esports**: Esports is another area where real-time scheduling and database management systems play a crucial role in online gaming. In esports, players compete against each other in organized tournaments. Real-time scheduling systems manage the tournament schedule and ensure that all matches start on time. Database management systems store player and team information, tournament results, and other relevant data, providing the necessary information to players and spectators.

4.4 Environmental Monitoring

Real-time databases are used in environmental monitoring systems for collecting, processing, and analyzing time-sensitive data related to weather, air quality, water quality, and other environmental factors [5]. Environmental monitoring is a critical process that involves collecting data on various environmental parameters to ensure that environmental conditions remain within acceptable levels. Real-time scheduling and database management systems are essential in environmental monitoring to ensure data is collected, stored, and analyzed accurately and efficiently.

Several issues related to environmental monitoring have been studied:

1. **Data collection and resource allocation**: Real-time scheduling systems are used in environmental monitoring to schedule data collection and allocate resources such as sensors and monitoring devices. These systems prioritize incoming requests based on the data's importance and urgency. Real-time scheduling systems manage the availability of resources, including bandwidth, CPU, and memory, ensuring that all devices collect data effectively. These systems also help load balancing, where the traffic load is spread evenly across different devices to prevent the overloading of a particular device. These databases must handle large volumes of data while ensuring that the data is consistent and reliable. In addition, the data is usually stored in real-time, allowing for rapid analysis and decision-making.

2. **Air quality monitoring**: One of the most common applications of real-time scheduling and database management systems in environmental monitoring is air quality monitoring. Air quality monitoring systems collect data on parameters such as particulate matter, carbon monoxide, and ozone. Real-time scheduling systems collect data and allocate resources such as sensors and monitoring devices. Database management systems store the collected data and provide analysis and decision-making tools. These systems can identify sources of pollution, track air quality trends over time, and provide information to policymakers and the public.

3. **Water monitoring**: This is another area where real-time scheduling and database management systems are crucial in environmental monitoring. Water quality monitoring systems collect data on parameters such as pH, temperature, humidity, wind speed, dissolved oxygen, and conductivity, among others. Real-time scheduling systems collect data and allocate resources such as sensors and monitoring devices. Database management systems store the collected data and provide analysis and decision-making tools. These systems can identify sources of contamination, track water quality trends over time, and provide information to policymakers and the public. Real-time scheduling systems collect data and allocate resources such as sensors and monitoring devices. Database management systems store the collected data and provide analysis and decision-making tools. These systems can provide accurate and timely weather forecasts, track weather patterns over time, and provide information to emergency responders and the public.

4. **Energy management**: Another area where real-time scheduling and database management systems are used in environmental monitoring is energy management. These systems monitor energy usage in buildings and industrial facilities, collecting data on parameters such as electricity, gas, and water usage. Real-time scheduling systems allocate resources such as sensors and monitoring devices, while database management systems store the collected data and provide analysis and decision-making tools. These systems can identify areas of energy waste, track energy usage trends over time, and provide information to facility managers and policymakers.

4.5 Sensor Network Applications

Sensor networks are a natural application for real-time data services because their primary purpose is to provide sensed data to some requesting entity, often with real-time constraints on the data and the requests [82].

Sensor networks are large-scale wireless networks that consist of numerous sensor and actuator nodes used to monitor and interact with physical environments [27]. From one perspective, sensor networks are similar to distributed database systems. They store environmental data on distributed nodes and respond to aperiodic and long-lived periodic queries [16]. Furthermore, data interest can be pre-registered

to the sensor network to collect and transmit the corresponding data only when needed. These specified interests are similar to views in traditional databases because they filter the data according to the application's data semantics and shield the overwhelming volume of raw data from applications [16].

Many issues of interest are related to sensor network applications that use real-time databases:

1. **Real-Time properties**: Sensor networks have inherent real-time properties. The environment that sensor networks interact with is usually dynamic and volatile. The sensor data typically have an absolute validity interval, after which the data values may not be consistent with the real environment. Transmitting and processing "stale" data wastes communication resources and can result in wrong decisions based on the reported out-of-date data. Besides data freshness, the data must often be sent to the destination by a deadline. Not much research has been performed on real-time data services in sensor networks.

2. **Differences with conventional RTDBMS**: Despite their similarity to conventional distributed real-time databases, sensor networks differ in the following ways. First, individual sensors are small in size and have limited computing resources, while they must also operate for long periods of time in an unattended fashion. This makes power conservation an essential concern in prolonging the system's lifetime. In current sensor networks, the primary source of power consumption is communication. To reduce unnecessary data transmission from each node, data collection and transmission in sensor networks are always initiated by subscriptions or queries. Second, any individual sensor is not reliable. Sensors can be damaged or die after consuming the energy in the battery. The wireless communication medium is also unreliable. Packets can collide or be lost. Because of these issues, we must build trust in a group of sensor nodes instead of any single node. Previous research emphasizes the reliable transmission of critical data or control packets at the lower levels. Still, more emphasis is needed on the reliability of data semantics at the higher level [83]. Third, the large amount of sensed data produced in sensor networks necessitates in-network processing. If all raw data is sent to base stations for further processing, the volume and burstiness of the traffic may cause many collisions and contribute to significant power loss. To minimize unnecessary data transmission, intermediate nodes or nearby nodes work together to filter and aggregate data before the data arrives at the destination. Fourth, sensor networks can interact with the environment by sensing and acting. When certain conditions are met, actuators can initiate an action on the environment. Since such actions are difficult to undo, reducing false alarms is crucial in specific applications.

3. **Middleware**: Many ongoing data service middleware research projects for the sensor network applications include Cougar, Rutgers Dataman, SINA, SCADDS, Smart-msgs, and some virtual-machine-like designs (Cougar Project; Dataman Project; SCADDS; Smart-msgs; [17, 30, 67, 93]. COUGAR and SINA are two typical data-centric middleware designs with goals similar to our design goal of providing data services. In COUGAR, sensor data is viewed as tables and query execution plans are developed and possibly optimized in the middleware.

DSWare project [59] is more tailored to sensor networks, including supporting group-based decisions, reliable data-centric storage, and implementing other approaches to improve the performance of real-time execution, reliability of aggregated results, and reduction of communication. SINA is a cluster-based middleware design that focuses on cooperating with sensors to conduct a task. Its extensive SQL-like primitives can be used to issue queries in sensor networks. However, it must provide schemes to hide the faulty nature of sensor operations and wireless communication. In SINA, the application layer must provide robustness and reliability for data services. The real-time scheduling component and built-in real-time features of other service components make DSWare more suitable than SINA for real-time applications in wireless sensor networks.

4. **Data fusion**: Multisensor data fusion research focuses on solutions that fuse data from multiple sensors to estimate the environment better [44, 77]. In mobile-agent-based data fusion approaches, software aggregating sensor information is packed and dispatched as mobile agents to "hot" areas (e.g., the area where an event occurred) and works independently there. The software migrates among sensors in a cluster, collects observations, then infers the real situation. This group-based approach uses consensus among several nearby sensors of the same type to increase the reliability of a single observation. The mobile agent-based approach, however, leverages the migration traffic of mobile agents and their appropriate processing at each sensor node in its routes. For instance, if a node in the route inserts incorrect data or refuses to forward the mobile agents, the aggregation and subsequent analysis are untrustful.

A fuzzy modeling approach is sometimes used for data fusion in sensor networks. It models the uncertainty in sensor failures and faulty observations [88]. This approach helps model the sensor error rates due to equipment wear and aggregating local decisions from multiple sensors that measure the same data type. In addition, some optimal decision schemes focus on the fusion of asynchronously arriving decisions [21, 87].

The work in [18] presents an approach for modeling and simulation for a real-time algorithm in multi-source data fusion systems. These data fusion schemes are suitable for increasing the accuracy of decisions but require extensive computing resources. Dempster-Shafer's evidential theory is also applied to incorporate uncertainty into decisions in some sensor fusion research. This scheme uses belief and plausibility functions to describe the reliability feature of each source and uses a normalized Dempster's combination rule to integrate decisions from different sources. The confidence function in DSWare is similar to the Dempster-Shafer method, except that it places the evidence in both temporal and spatial spectrums to consider the real-time validity intervals of data and possible contexts.

4.6 Web-based Real-Time Data Services

Another application that has recently become a subject of research is real-time web-based data services [82].

Real-time DBMSs play a crucial role in web-based real-time data services by providing efficient and reliable data storage and management. These database systems are designed to handle high volumes of data with strict timing constraints, ensuring that real-time updates are delivered to users in a timely manner. By integrating real-time DBMS into web-based services, developers can create applications that deliver real-time data updates, enable collaborative features, and support interactive user experiences.

The World Wide Web has recently offered a new venue for real-time data services. Many applications, such as program stock trading, require information services that can provide real-time data to widely distributed users. The main challenge in these applications is to provide timely access to new data in the face of the highly dynamic environment of the web. Due to the unpredictable nature of web-based applications, most of this area's research has focused on providing QoS management for real-time data services. In [89], a web-based content distribution service for industrial applications is presented. The service allows for remote monitoring of industrial devices that may be geographically distributed. It is based on an active web caching architecture that provides on-demand replication of dynamically changing web content, like industrial process state. The active web cache comprises a standard web proxy cache that handles all static data and an active server that handles one or more dynamic content types. The approach of [89] is to trade off temporal data consistency with timeliness while keeping within specified inconsistency bounds.

Main benefits of Real-Time DBMS in Web-Based Services are the following:

1. **Real-Time Data Updates**: Real-time DBMSs enable instant updates to be delivered to users, ensuring that they have access to the latest information. This is especially important in applications such as real-time chat, collaborative editing, and real-time analytics, where data accuracy and timeliness are critical.
2. **Data Synchronization**: Real-time DBMSs facilitate seamless data synchronization across multiple devices and users. Changes made by one user are immediately propagated to others, ensuring consistency and avoiding conflicts in shared data. This capability is essential in collaborative applications and multi-user environments.
3. **Scalability**: Web-based real-time data services often experience high user loads and concurrent data updates. Real-time DBMSs are designed to handle scalability requirements, allowing applications to scale horizontally or vertically to accommodate growing user bases and increasing data volumes.
4. **Performance**: Real-time DBMSs are optimized for low-latency data access and fast query processing. This ensures that web-based applications can retrieve and present real-time data to users without noticeable delays, providing a smooth and responsive user experience.

Besides the applications described above, other applications of Real-Time DBMS in Web-Based Services are the following:

1. **Real-Time Collaboration**: Real-time DBMSs are extensively used in collaborative web applications such as project management tools, document editing platforms, and virtual whiteboards. They enable multiple users to work simultaneously, seeing each other's changes in real-time.

2. **Live Dashboards and Analytics**: Real-time DBMSs power web-based analytics dashboards that provide real-time insights and visualizations. This is particularly useful in domains such as stock market monitoring, website analytics, and real-time performance monitoring.

3. **Real-Time Messaging and Notifications**: Real-time DBMSs underpin web-based messaging applications, enabling instant messaging, chatbots, and push notifications. These services deliver real-time messages and updates to users, ensuring timely communication.

4. **Real-Time Gaming**: Real-time DBMSs are essential in web-based multiplayer gaming applications, facilitating real-time game state synchronization, leaderboard management, and real-time interactions between players.

5. **IoT Data Management**: Web-based services that integrate with Internet of Things (IoT) devices rely on real-time DBMSs to handle the massive influx of sensor data in real-time. These services can collect, process, and visualize real-time data from IoT devices, enabling applications such as smart home automation, asset tracking, and environmental monitoring.

By leveraging the capabilities of real-time DBMSs, web-based real-time data services can deliver dynamic, interactive, and synchronized experiences to users. They enable real-time collaboration, data visualization, messaging, gaming, and IoT data management. The combination of web technologies and real-time DBMSs opens up a world of possibilities for creating engaging and responsive web-based applications that cater to real-time data processing and synchronization demands.

References

1. Abad, P., Fekete, A.D., Lee, B.S.: Adaptive two-phase commit for real-time distributed database systems. Concurrency and Computation: Practice and Experience **21**(9), 1123–1142 (2009)
2. Abbott, R., Garcia-Molina, H.: Scheduling real-time transactions: A performance evaluation. ACM Transactions on Database Systems **17**(3), 513–560 (1992)
3. Abbott, R.K., Garcia-Molina, H.: Scheduling real-time transactions: A performance evaluation. ACM Trans. Database Syst. **17**(3), 513–560 (1992). DOI 10.1145/132271.132276. URL http://doi.acm.org/10.1145/132271.132276
4. Abbott, R.K., Garcia-Molina, H.: Scheduling i/o requests with deadlines: a performance evaluation. In: Proceedings of the 1993 ACM SIGMETRICS conference on Measurement and modeling of computer systems, pp. 113–124 (1993)
5. Acevedo, M.F.: Real-Time Environmental Monitoring: Sensors and Systems. CRC Press (2018)
6. Adelberg, B., Kao, B., Garcia-Molina, H.: Overview of the stanford real-time information processor (strip). SIGMOD Rec. **25**(1), 34–37 (1996). DOI 10.1145/381854.381882. URL http://doi.acm.org/10.1145/381854.381882
7. Adeli, H., Wu, Y.: Recovery in real-time database systems. In: Pacific Rim International Symposium on Fault-Tolerant Systems, pp. 2–7. IEEE (1992)
8. Ahmad, H., Dharmadasa, I., Ullah, F., Babar, M.A.: A review on c3i systems' security: Vulnerabilities attacks and countermeasures. ACM Computing Surveys **55**(9), 192 (2023). DOI 10.1145/3558001. Article No.: 1-38
9. Amirijoo, M., Chaufette, N., Hansson, J., Son, S.H., Gunnarsson, S.: Generalized performance management of multi-class real-time imprecise data services. In: Proceedings of the 26th IEEE International Real-Time Systems Symposium, RTSS '05, pp. 38–49. IEEE Computer Society, Washington DC USA (2005). DOI 10.1109/RTSS.2005.23. URL http://dx.doi.org/10.1109/RTSS.2005.23
10. Andreoli, R., Cucinotta, T., Pedreschi, D.: Rt-mongodb: A nosql database with differentiated performance. In: Proceedings of the 11th International Conference on Cloud Computing and Services Science (CLOSER 2021), pp. 77–86 (2021). DOI 10.5220/0010452400770086
11. Ara, G., Abeni, L., Cucinotta, T., Vitucci, C.: On the use of kernel bypass mechanisms for high-performance inter-container communications. In: High Performance Computing, pp. 1–12. Springer International Publishing (2019)
12. Baruah, S., Bertogna, M., Buttazzo, G.: Multiprocessor Scheduling for Real-Time Systems. Springer International Publishing (2015)
13. Bernstein, P.A., Goodman, N.: Multiversion concurrency control theory and algorithms. ACM Trans. Database Systems. **8**(4), 465–483 (1983)
14. Bernstein, P.A., Hadzilacos, V., Goodman, N.: Concurrency Control and Recovery in Database Systems. Addison-Wesley Longman Publishing Co. Inc., Boston MA. USA (1987)
15. Bestavros, A.: Deterministic modeling of real-time transaction systems. Journal of Real-Time Systems **7**(3), 279–303 (1994)
16. Bonnet, P., Gehrke, J., Seshadri, P.: Querying the physical world. IEEE Personal Communications Maganize **10 15** (2000)
17. Bonnet, P., Gehrke, J., Seshadri, P.: Towards sensor database systems. In: Proceedings of the 2nd International Conference on Mobile Data Management. Hong Kong. (2001)
18. Bosse, E., Roy, J., Paradis, S.: Modeling and simulation in support of design of a data fusion system. Information Fusion **1**, 77–87 (2000)
19. Bradley, S.A.: Strip: A soft real-time main memory database for open systems. Ph.D. thesis (1997)
20. Buttazzo, G., Lipari, G., Abeni, L., Caccamo, M.: Soft real-time systems: Predictability vs. efficiency. Springer US (2005)
21. Chang, W., Kam, M.: Asynchronous distributed detection. IEEE Transactions on Aerospace Electronic Systems. pp. 818–826 (1994)

© The Author(s), under exclusive license to Springer Nature Switzerland AG 2024
P. Mejia Alvarez et al., *Real-Time Database Systems*, SpringerBriefs in Computer Science,
https://doi.org/10.1007/978-3-031-44230-8

22. Chen, Y.C., Makki, K., Mendelzon, A.O.: Dynamic buffer management for real-time database systems. In: Proceedings of the 16th International Conference on Very Large Data Bases, pp. 438–449. VLDB Endowment (1990)
23. Consortium, S.: Sqlite - a high-reliability embedded zero-configuration public-domain sql database engine (2023). URL https://www.sqlite.org/. [Online; accessed 27-April-2023]
24. Devor, C., Carlson, C.: Structural locking mechanisms and their effect on database management system performance. Inf. Syst. **7**(4), 345–358 (1982). DOI 10.1016/0306-4379(82) 90033-3. URL https://doi.org/10.1016/0306-4379(82)90033-3
25. DiPippo, L.C., Sventek, R., Hong, J., Wolfe, V.F.: Reintegration in distributed real-time systems. In: Proceedings of the IEEE Real-Time Systems Symposium, pp. 144–154 (1998)
26. Elmasri, R., Wuu, G., Kim, Y.: Efficient techniques for fuzzy and partial checkpointing in main memory database systems. In: Proceedings of the IEEE 6th International Conference on Data Engineering, pp. 588–595 (1990)
27. Estrin, D.G., Heidemann, R.J., Kumar, S.: Next century challenges: scalable coordination in sensor networks. In: Proceedings of the 5th Annual International Conference on Mobile Computing and Networks (1999)
28. ExtremeDB-RT: Extremedb-rt. https://www.mcobject.com/docs/Content/Appendix/RT.htm
29. Fekete, A.D., Lynch, N.A., Shavit, N.: Real-time 3pc: A new commit protocol with a strict real-time ordering. Proceedings of the 9th Annual ACM Symposium on Principles of Distributed Computing pp. 39–49 (1990)
30. Feng, J., Koushanfar, F., Potkonjak, M.: System-architectures for sensor networks: issues alternatives and directions. In: The 20th International Conference on Computer Design. Freiburg Germany. (2001)
31. Gopalan, K., Natarajan, A., Dwarkadas, S., Scott, M.L., Strum, M.: Effective buffer cache management for real-time database systems. In: 2003 Symposium on Applications and the Internet Workshops (SAINT 2003. Workshops), pp. 260–267. IEEE (2003)
32. Grey, J., A., R.: Transaction Processing: Concepts and Techniques. Morgan Kaufman (1992)
33. Guo, S., Zhang, Z., Guo, M., Wang, J., Qian, G.: Performance optimization for real-time databases on ssds. Journal of Systems Architecture **97**, 205–217 (2019)
34. Haritsa, J.R., Carey, M.J., Livny, M.: On being optimistic about real-time constraints. In: Proceedings of the Ninth ACM SIGACT-SIGMOD-SIGART Symposium on Principles of Database Systems, PODS '90, pp. 331–343. ACM, New York NY USA (1990). DOI 10.1145/298514.298585. URL http://doi.acm.org/10.1145/298514.298585
35. Haritsa, J.R., Ramamritham, K., Gupta, R.: Real-time databases: problems solutions and future directions. In: 1991 International Conference on Information Engineering, pp. 42–49. IEEE (1991)
36. Haritsa, J.R., Ramamritham, K., Stankovic, J.A.: Real-time locking protocols. In: Proceedings of the 11th Real-Time Systems Symposium, pp. 144–153. IEEE (1990)
37. Haritsa Jayant, R.: Real-time concurrency control protocols. The VLDB Journal **9**(1), 60–79 (2000)
38. Huang, J., Stankovic, J.A., Ramamritham, K., Towsley, D.: On using priority inheritance in real-time databases. Tech. rep., Amherst MA USA (1990)
39. Huang, J.W.S.: Concurrency control in real-time databases. In: Proceedings of the 7th International Conference on Data Engineering, pp. 530–539. IEEE (1991)
40. Huang, T.W., Tsai, Y.C., Cheng, A.C.: Adaptive real-time buffer management for mixed hard and soft real-time systems. Real-Time Systems **19**(2), 127–153 (2000)
41. Huang, W., Jajodia, S., Mutchler, D.: A real-time two-phase commit protocol. In: Proceedings of the 1991 ACM SIGMOD international conference on Management of data, pp. 41–50. ACM (1991)
42. Hwang, K., Kim, C.: Fault tolerance and recovery in real-time database systems. Information and Software Technology **43**(12), 713–723 (2001)
43. Ioannou, P.A., Sun, J.: Adaptive control tutorial. Siam (2012)

44. Jayasimha, D., Ivengar, S., Kashyap, R.: Information integration and synchronization in distributed sensor networks. IEEE Transactions on Systems Man and Cybernetics. **21**(5), 1032–1043 (1991)
45. Kamath, M., Ramamritham, K.: Priority-driven buffer management for real-time main-memory database systems. Real-Time Systems **5**(1), 37–76 (1993)
46. Kang, K., Oh, J., Son, S.: Chronos: Feedback control of a real database system performance. In: 28th IEEE International Real-Time Systems Symposium (RTSS 2007), pp. 267–276 (2007). DOI 10.1109/RTSS.2007.16
47. Kang, K., Son, S., Stankovic, J.: Qedb: A quality-aware embedded real-time database. In: Proceedings of the 9th IEEE Real-Time and Embedded Technology and Applications Symposium, pp. 70–79. IEEE (2003)
48. Kang, K.D., Sin, P.H., Oh, J.: A real-time database testbed and performance evaluation. In: Proceedings of the 13th IEEE International Conference on Embedded and Real-Time Computing Systems and Applications, RTCSA '07, pp. 319–326. IEEE Computer Society, Washington DC USA (2007). DOI 10.1109/RTCSA.2007.12. URL http://dx.doi.org/10.1109/RTCSA.2007.12
49. Kang, K.D., Son, S.H., Stankovic, J.A.: Managing deadline miss ratio and sensor data freshness in real databases. IEEE Transactions on Knowledge and Data Engineering **16**(10), 1200–1216 (2004)
50. Kang, M., Son, S.H.: Adaptive real-time database management systems for internet of things. Future Generation Computer Systems **82**, 696–705 (2018)
51. Kao, B., Garcia-Molina, H.: An overview of real-time database systems. In: Advances in Real-Time Systems, pp. 463–486. Springer-Verlag (1994)
52. Korth, H.F., Soparkar, N., Silberschatz, A.: Triggered real-time databases with consistency constraints. In: Proceedings of the 16th International Conference on Very Large Data Bases, VLDB '90, pp. 71–82. Morgan Kaufmann Publishers Inc., San Francisco CA USA (1990). URL http://dl.acm.org/citation.cfm?id=645916.671972
53. Krol, V., Pokorny, J.: The v4db testbed - evaluating of real-time database transaction processing strategies testbed- evaluating of real-time database transaction processing strategies. In: Proceedings of the 11th WSEAS International Conference on Computers (2007)
54. Kuo, T.W., Kao, Y., Kuo, C.: Two-version based concurrency control and recovery in real-time client/server databases. IEEE Transactions on Computers **52**(4), 506–524 (2003). DOI 10.1109/TC.2003.1190591
55. Kuo, T.W., Mok, A.K.: Real-time database — similarity and resource scheduling. SIGMOD Rec. **25**(1), 18–22 (1996). DOI 10.1145/381854.381873. URL http://doi.acm.org/10.1145/381854.381873
56. Lam, K., Kuo, T.W. (eds.): Real-Time database systems: architecture and techniques. Kluwer Academic Plublishers (2001)
57. Lee, Y., Lee, B.S.: A priority-based commit protocol for real-time distributed database systems. In: Proceedings 2000 International Database Engineering and Applications Symposium, pp. 20–29. IEEE (2000)
58. Lettieri, G., Maffione, V., Rizzo, L.: A survey of fast packet i/o technologies for network function virtualization. In: Lecture Notes in Computer Science, pp. 579–590. Springer International Publishing (2017)
59. Li, S., Lin, Y., Son, S.H., Stankovic, J., Wei, Y.: Event detection services using data service middleware in distributed sensor networks. Telecommunication Systems. **26**, 351–368 (2004)
60. Lin, E.S., Ramamritham, K.: Adaptive deadlines for real-time disk scheduling. Real-Time Systems **18**(1), 7–41 (2000)
61. Lin, K.J., Lin, M.J.: Enhancing availability in distributed real-time databases. SIGMOD Rec. **17**(1), 34–43 (1988). DOI 10.1145/44203.44206. URL http://doi.acm.org/10.1145/44203.44206
62. Lin, Y., Son, S.: Concurrency control in real-time databases by dynamic adjustment of serialization order. In: Proceedings 11th Real-Time Systems Symposium, pp. 104–112 (1990). DOI 10.1109/REAL.1990.128735

63. Lindström, J.: Wiley Encyclopedia of Computer Science and Engineering, chap. Real Time Database Systems. Wiley (2008)
64. Liu, C.L., Layland, J.W.: Scheduling algorithms for multiprogramming in a hard-real-time environment. Journal of the ACM **20**(1), 46–61 (1973)
65. Locke, D.: Real-Time Database Systems: Architecture and Techniques, chap. Applications and System Characteristics. Kluwer Academic Plublishers (2001)
66. Lu, C., Abdelzaher, T.F., Stankovic, J.A., Son, S.H.: Feedback control real-time scheduling: Framework, modeling, and algorithms. Real-Time Systems **23**(1-2), 85–126 (2001)
67. Mattern, F., Romer, K., Kasten, O.: Middleware challenges for wireless sensor networks. ACM SIGMOBILE Mobile Computing and Communication Review (2002)
68. Meehan, W., Brook, R.G., Wyland, J.: Geographic Information Systems in Energy and Utilities, pp. 755–779. Springer International Publishing (2022). DOI 10.1007/978-3-030-53125-6_28. URL https://doi.org/10.1007/978-3-030-53125-6_28
69. Mohan, C., Haderle, D., Lindsay, B., Pirahesh, H., Schwarz, P.: Aries: A transaction recovery method supporting fine-granularity locking and partial rollbacks using write-ahead logging. ACM Transactions on Database Systems **17**(1), 94–162 (1992)
70. Nguyen, D.: Raima database manager version 15.2 architecture and features (2022). URL https://raima.com/wp-content/uploads/Technical-Whitepaper.pdf. Accessed: May 2023
71. Nystrom, D., Tesanovic, A., Nolin, N., Hansson, J.: Comet: A component-based realtime database for automotive systems. In: Proceedings of the IEEE Workshop on Software Engineering for Automotive Systems (2004)
72. Ongaro, D., Ousterhout, J.: In search of an understandable consensus algorithm (extended version). Tech. rep. (2016). Accessed 20:2018
73. Palanisamy, S., SuvithaVani, P.: A survey on rdbms and nosql databases mysql vs mongodb. In: 2020 International Conference on Computer Communication and Informatics (ICCCI), pp. 1–7 (2020)
74. Pang, H., Carey, M.: Predictive dynamic real-time admission control. IEEE Transactions on Knowledge and Data Engineering vol. 11 no. 1 pp. 184–198 (1999)
75. Paton, N.W., Díaz, O.: Active database systems. ACM Computing Surveys **31**(1), 63–103 (1999)
76. Pu, C., Leff, A., Raynal, M.: Epsilon-serializability. ACM Transactions on Database Systems (TODS) **16**(3), 492–525 (1991)
77. Qi, H., Wang, X., Iyengar, S.S., Chakrabarty, K.: Multisensor data fusion in distributed sensor networks using mobile agents. In: Proceedings of 5th International Conference on Information Fusion. Annapolis MD. (2001)
78. Ramamritham, K.: Real-time databases. International Journal of Distributed and Parallel Databases, Springer **1**, 199–226 (1993)
79. Ramamritham, K., Haritsa, J.: Real-time database systems: Issues and applications. IEEE Expert: Intelligent Systems and Their Applications **8**(1), 26–38 (1993)
80. Ramamritham, K., Liu, Q.: Adaptive push-pull: Disseminating dynamic web data. In: Proceedings of the 10th International Conference on World Wide Web, pp. 265–274. ACM (2001)
81. Ramamritham, K., Singhal, M.: Real-time scheduling of disk i/o in a multi-tasking environment. In: Proceedings of the 1989 ACM SIGMETRICS Conference on Measurement and Modeling of Computer Systems, pp. 53–62. ACM (1989)
82. Ramanritahm, K., Son, S.H., Cingiser, D.L.: Real-time databases and data services. Real-Time Systems Journal **28**, 179–215 (2004)
83. Ratnasamy, S., Estrin, D., Govindan, R., Karp, B., Shenker, S., Yin, L., Yu, F.: Data-centric storage in sensornets. In: Proceedings of the 1st Workshop on Sensor Networks and Applications (2002)
84. Rawlings, J.B., Mayne, D.Q., Scokaert, P.O.: Model Predictive Control: Theory, Computation, and Design. Nob Hill Pub (2017)
85. Rubio, F., Vazquez, P., Reyes, C.R.P.: Nosql vs. sql in big data management: An empirical study. KnE Engineering **5**(1), 40–49 (2020)

86. Safadinho, D., Ramos, J., Ribeiro, R., Caetano, R., Pereira, A.: Uav multiplayer platform for real-time online gaming. In: A. Rocha, A.M. Correia, H. Adeli, L.P. Reis, S. Costanzo (eds.) Recent Advances in Information Systems and Technologies, pp. 577–585. Springer International Publishing (2017)
87. Samarasooriya, V.N.S., Varshney, P.K.: A sequential approach to asynchronous decision fusion. Optical Engineering. **35(3)**, 625–633 (1996)
88. Samarasooriya, V.N.S., Varshney, P.K.: A fuzzy modeling approach to decision fusion under uncertainty. Fuzzy Sets and Systems. **114(1)**, 59–69 (2000)
89. Sebastine, S., Kang, K.D., Abdelzaher, T., Son, S.H.: A scalable web-based real-time information distribution service for industrial applications. In: Proceedings of the 27th Annual Conference of IEEE Industrial Electronics Society. Denver CO. (2001)
90. Sha, L., Rajkumar, R., Lehoczky, J.P.: Priority inheritance protocols: An approach to real-time synchronization. IEEE Transactions on Computers **39**(9), 1175–1185 (1990)
91. Sha, L., Rajkumar, R., Son, S., Chun-Hyon, C.: A real-time locking protocol. Tech. Rep. CMU/SEI-89-TR-018, Software Engineering Institute Carnegie Mellon University, Pittsburgh PA (1989). URL http://resources.sei.cmu.edu/library/asset-view.cfm?AssetID=10955
92. Shahzad, M., Ahmad, I.: Real-time systems object-relational active database (rtsorac): A real-time object-oriented database model. International Journal of Real-Time Systems **1**(1), 1–15 (2021)
93. Shen, C.C., Srisathapornphat, C., Jaikaeo, C.: Sensor information networking architecture and applications. IEEE Personal Communication Magazine. **8(4)**, 52–59 (2001)
94. Shu, W., Huang, Y., Zheng, W., Ravindran, B., Jensen, E.D.: A real-time two-phase commit protocol for distributed real-time database systems. In: Proceedings of the IEEE Real-Time Systems Symposium, pp. 422–432 (1999)
95. Sivasankaran, M., Stankovic, J., Towsley, D., Ramamritham, K., Purimet, l.B.: Epsilon serializability. In: Proceedings of the IEEE Real-Time Systems Symposium, pp. 56–65 (1995)
96. Sivasankaran, R., Son, S.H.: Real-time recovery: A taxonomy and a performance study. Journal of Real-Time Systems **18**(1), 5–37 (2000)
97. Son, S., Kim, S.: Real-time database systems: Issues and applications. IEEE Transactions on Knowledge and Data Engineering **12**(2), 181–200 (2000)
98. Son, S.H.: A timing constraint approach to object-oriented databases. ACM SIGMOD Record **30**(4), 64–69 (2001)
99. Son, S.H., Iannacone, C.C., Poris, M.S.: Rtdb: a real-time database manager for time-critical applications. In: Proceedings. EUROMICRO '91 Workshop on Real-Time Systems, pp. 207–214 (1991). DOI 10.1109/EMWRT.1991.144107
100. Son, S.H., Kim, K.H.: A real-time two-phase commit protocol. International Journal of Parallel and Distributed Systems and Networks **5**(1), 38–45 (1995)
101. Son, S.H., Krishna, C.M.: An adaptive recovery technique for real-time database systems. In: Proceedings of the IEEE Real-Time Technology and Applications Symposium, pp. 98–106 (1998)
102. Son, S.H., Zhang, F.: A real-time optimistic concurrency control protocol with dynamic adjustment of serialization order. IEEE Transactions on Knowledge and Data Engineering **18**(6), 838–850 (2006)
103. Stankovic, J., Son, H.S., Hansson, J.: Misconceptions about real-time databases. IEEE Computer **32**, 29–36 (1999)
104. Stankovic, J.A., Ramamritham, K.: Tutorial: Real-time systems. IEEE Computer Society Press (1988)
105. Stankovic, J.A., Ramamritham, K.: The design of dynamic real-time scheduling algorithms. pp. pp. 59–70 (1989)
106. Stankovic, J.A., Son, S.H., Liebeherr, J.: BeeHive: Global Multimedia Database Support for Dependable Real-Time Applications, pp. 51–69. Springer Berlin Heidelberg (1998)
107. Sugeno, M.: Industrial applications of fuzzy control. Elsevier Science Inc. (1985)

108. Tatbul, N., Çetintemel, U., Zdonik, S.B., Cherniack, M., Stonebraker, M.: Load shedding in a data stream manager. In: VLDB'03: Proceedings of the 29th International Conference on Very Large Data Bases, pp. 309–320. VLDB Endowment (2003)

109. Tesanovic, A.: Reconfigurable real-time software using aspects and components. Ph.D. thesis (2006)

110. Tesanovic, A., Hansson, J.: Application-Taylored Databases for Real-Time Systems, pp. 28.1–28.19. Chapman and Hall/CRC (2008)

111. Tesanovic, A., Nadjm-Tehrani, S., Hansson, J.: Component-Based Software Development for Embedded Systems - An Overview on Current Research Trends, pp. 59–81. Springer-Verlag Lecture notes in Computer Science Volume 3778 (2005)

112. Tesanovic, A., Nystrom, J.H., Norstrom, C.: Integrating symbolic worst-case execution time analysis into aspect-oriented software development. In: OOPSLA 2002 Workshop on Tools for Aspect Oriented Software Development (2002)

113. Ulusoy, O.: Real-time concurrency control in database systems. In: Proceedings of the IEEE Workshop on Real-Time Applications, pp. 38–42 (1993)

114. Vrbsky, S., Liu, J.: Soft real-time concurrency control. Journal of Real-Time Systems $10(1)$, 5–39 (1996)

115. Wang, X., Stankovic, J.A., Lu, C.: Dynamic resource allocation for distributed real-time systems. In: Proceedings of the 12th Euromicro Conference on Real-Time Systems, pp. 17–24. IEEE (2002)

116. Wu, Q., Li, Q., Wang, C., Zhao, S., Yu, G.: A deep reinforcement learning-based i/o scheduler for real-time database systems. In: 2019 IEEE 39th International Conference on Distributed Computing Systems (ICDCS), pp. 1180–1190. IEEE (2019)

117. Yao, B., Butt, A.R., Wang, K.J.: A new approach to i/o scheduling for real-time database systems. ACM Transactions on Database Systems (TODS) $20(3)$, 273–320 (1995)

118. Zhang, C., Liu, Z., Qi, Y., Wang, Z., He, J., Wen, J.: Machine learning-based i/o scheduler for real-time database systems. Journal of Systems Architecture 88, 55–65 (2018)

119. Zheng, L., Zhou, M., Son, S.H.: A machine learning-based real-time commit protocol for distributed real-time database systems. In: 2017 IEEE 37th International Conference on Distributed Computing Systems (ICDCS), pp. 1668–1678. IEEE (2017)

120. Zhu, X., Chiueh, T.c.: Pattern-based buffer cache management. In: Proceedings. Eighth International Symposium on High-Performance Computer Architecture, pp. 147–156. IEEE (2002)

Printed in the United States
by Baker & Taylor Publisher Services